Other titles published by Texas Fish & Game Publishing

BOOKS:

KAYAK Texas
by Greg Berlocher

TEXAS Waterfowl
by Chester Moore, Jr.

THE Texas Deer Book
by Steve LaMascus & Greg Rodriguez

Saltwater Strategies®: Flounder Fever
by Chester Moore, Jr.

Saltwater Strategies®: Where, When & How to Wadefish Texas
by Bink Grimes

Freshwater Strategies®: A Practical Approach to Texas Freshwater Fishing
by Doug Pike

Saltwater Strategies®: Texas Reds
by Chester Moore, Jr.

Saltwater Strategies®: Texas Trout Tactics
by Chester Moore, Jr.

Saltwater Strategies®: Pat Murray's No-Nonsense Guide to Coastal Fishing
by Pat Murray

Texas Saltwater Classics: Fly Patterns for the Texas Coast
by Greg Berlocher

Doreen's 24 Hour Eat Gas Now Café
by Reavis Z. Wortham

PERIODICALS:
Texas Fish & Game Magazine (12x/year)
Texas Lakes & Bays Atlas (annual)

Order by phone: 1-800-750-4678 or online: www.fishgame.com

Texas Fish & Game's
Saltwater Strategies™ Book Series
presents

TEXAS TROUT TACTICS

by Chester Moore, Jr.

Texas Fish & Game
Publishing Co., L.L.C.

1745 Greens Road
Houston, Texas 77032
1-800-750-4678
www.fishgame.com

Although the author and publisher have extensively researched all brand names and sources to ensure the accuracy and completeness of information in this book, we assume no responsibility for errors, inaccuracies, omissions or any other inconsistency herein. Any slights against people, products, manufacturers or organizations are unintentional.

Saltwater Strategies, Texas Trout Tactics, Copyright© 2009 by Texas Fish & Game Publishing Company, L.L.C. All rights reserved. No part of this book may be reproduced, stored in a retrieval system or transmitted in any form, by any type of electronic, mechanical or copy technique without the prior written permission of the publisher, except by a reviewer, who may quote brief passages in a review.

Published by
TEXAS FISH & GAME PUBLISHING CO., L.L.C.
1745 Greens Road
Houston Texas 77032
Phone: 281-227-3001 Fax: 281-227-3002
www.fishgame.com

Second Edition

Cover photo by George Knighten

Foreword by Doug Pike

Edited by Don Zaidle.

All photos by Chester Moore, Jr., unless otherwise credited.

Production and design by Wendy Kipfmiller

Cover art by Jimmy Borne

ISBN: 0-929980-08-5

DEDICATION

This book is dedicated to my daughter Faith. You are a true gift from God and I treasure you even more than my time in the great outdoors. Mommy and Daddy love you very much.

Contents

Foreword ix

Introduction xi

Chapter One 1
Biology: *Speckled trout biology, myths, and anglers' attitudes*

Chapter Two 17
Seasonal Patterns: *The best times and tactics for the seasons*

Chapter Three 51
Understanding Tides: *Why the moon and sun make a difference*

Chapter Four 61
Tackle: *Selecting rods, reels and line*

Chapter Five 75
Lures: *The allure of metal and plastic fakery*

Chapter Six 103
Live bait: *When all else fails—and even when it doesn't*

Chapter Seven 121
Fly-fishing: *The romantic side of speckled trout fishing*

Chapter Eight 131
Jetties: *hard rock trout cafes*

A Day in the Life of an Outdoor Writer

Many people wonder what it is like to be an outdoor writer. This photo gives you a little glimpse as author Chester Moore photographs Mark Davis in Lower Laguna Madre near Port Mansfield. Being an outdoor writer means often foregoing a rod and reel and using a camera. At times it can be difficult to do that but being able to put out quality work like this book makes it worthwhile. Plus, there are enough fishing opportunities to make a man happy. It is not all work.

Chapter Nine..............143
Short rig savvy: Striking trout where they drilled for oil

Chapter Ten.................155
Going to the bank: Cashing in on surf, pier and shoreline fishing

Chapter Eleven 169
Trout hotspots: Where the trout are

Chapter Twelve 187
Trout recipes, preparation, & preservation: From the bay to the table

Chapter Thirteen........201
Making book: Putting one in the record books

Chapter Fourteen........209
Supertrout: Will selective breeding and genetic engineering produce a speckled "frankenfish?"

Acknowledgment........217

Index..........................219

Foreword

Having known Chester Moore, Jr., for several years now, I have drawn two conclusions about him: He loves fishing, and he hates barbers.

The long hair and quiet demeanor never fooled me. Chester's fervor for the outdoors was apparent from the time I first shook his hand at an annual gathering of the Texas Outdoor Writers Association, and it has not waned since. I count him among a rare few in this profession who seem to have genuine passion for natural resources and the outdoors, a relationship that transcends simple respect. As he fishes, Chester's focus reaches beyond the end of the line.

It is that closeness to nature that enables Chester to write at length and in specific detail on catching speckled trout, one of the most popular sport fish on the entire Gulf Coast. The information he shares in *Saltwater Strategies: Trout Tactics* was gathered over many years and from countless sources. Through Chester, in a single package, readers gain access to the thoughts and opinions of trout fishing's top experts.

Chester's own expertise, as well, is evident throughout the book. Never one to sit back and take notes while others fished, he has spent thousands of hours "walking the walk" around the bay and beachfront. A true master on the subject in his own right, Chester manages to deliver his message in words and symbolism that every fisherman can understand and put to use on the water.

Saltwater Strategies: Trout Tactics is an excellent addition to any coastal angler's bookshelf. It reads smoothly and easily, like a casual conversation between friends—-one of which just happens to know a lot more about speckled trout fishing than the other.

Doug Pike
Houston, Texas

Introduction

Speckled trout *are* inland saltwater fishing along most of the Gulf Coast. No other species comes close in terms of angler interest, tackle industry focus, and evoking impassioned angler opinions.

When I was growing up in the early 1980s, redfish were the kings of the coast. They remain the favorites of many fishermen, but something happened along the way to elevate the speckled trout to super star status.

When I was a kid, the "redfish wars" had just wrapped up and the species was en route to recovery after decades of abuse from the commercial fishing industry. Catching a limit of legal-sized redfish in some areas was on par with hitting the lottery. That didn't happen often, and when it did, it meant something to the angler. I remember catching my first legal-sized redfish and thinking I was the coolest kid on the block. To this day, I carry a snapshot of me with that fish in a photo album.

Somewhere in that era, trout fishing started to gain momentum. Anglers became fascinated with using artificial lures to catch coastal fish and trout responded better than any other. No longer did they hit old standards like silver spoons and shrimp tails. They also hit lures designed for bass, such as lipless crankbaits and topwater plugs. Yes, *topwater plugs*. In my opinion, that's what took trout out of the shadows and put them in the spotlight. When anglers realized trout would readily hit topwater plugs, many traded in their bait buckets and popping corks for bass rods and Chug Bugs. A fishing revolution had begun and no one even knew it.

I first figured this out back in the late 1980s, when my father and I saw a guy sitting on the bank casting a big, wooden topwater plug into a marshy cut. We saw this man fishing all the time, but he usually had big surf rods set out for reds and garfish. "I'm a trout fisherman now," he said.

The speckled trout is to saltwater fishing as the largemouth bass is to freshwater. It is responsible for millions of dollars entering the economies of coastal communities, is the most popular species among artificial lure enthusiasts, and even keeps a couple of major tournament trails afloat. Yes, speckled trout have truly arrived.

In the spring of 2009, I had the pleasure of watching Texas Parks & Wildlife Department (TPWD) technicians with Sea Center Texas release speckled trout fingerlings into Keith Lake Cut near Sabine Lake. This was a special trip for me on a personal level, because I was one of the anglers who caught the parents of these fish during a special trout roundup. Proud Papa syndrome was in full effect as I watched the beautiful, tiny specks enter the water.

Then something caught my attention.

As the last few fish were netted from the bottom of the tank, it was obvious some were much bigger than others. Most were around an inch in length, while some were more 3 inches and as big around as my finger.

Could those big ones represent superior "super trout" genetics?

After talking with TPWD biologist Shane Bonnot, who oversees much of the broodstock harvest at Sea Center, I learned the answer is "maybe."

"On some of those stockings, we'll harvest fish from several ponds and sometimes we'll have slightly different age classes," Bonnot said. "However, sometimes we'll harvest fish from the ponds and most of them are about an inch long and sometimes we'll see some that are 3-4 inches long, and that is most likely from superior genetics. Some just get bigger, and do so quicker."

TPWD has done an amazing job enhancing the gene pool of largemouth bass through the Budweiser ShareLunker program, a program of selective breeding using females exceeding 13 pounds donated by anglers. Has coastal hatchery technology reached the point where super-sized specks

Introduction

Chester Moore signs copies of "Flounder Fundamentals" for his fans at a boat show.

can be hand picked for breeding to enhance the number of trophy trout in Texas bays?

"Through the Coastal Bay Teams events, we have taken donations of any trout and haven't really discriminated as to what we spawn, but it is definitely good to get big fish," Bonnot said. "We have went on special trips to get fish from different bay systems and caught some really big ones that have been spawned for stocking with special interest."

Through the ShareLunker program, TPWD biologists have learned much about soliciting donations of fish from the public, handling them for maximum survival rate, and using top genetics to benefit fisheries.

As predicted in the "Age of the SuperTrout" story I wrote for Texas Fish & Game back in 1999, TPWD fisheries managers have made great strides in genetic coding of speckled trout populations. They have determined that trout from Lower Laguna Madre cannot be stocked in Trinity Bay and vice-versa due to genetic differences. They have also made great strides in research methods that helped to determine these differences. TPWD coastal fisheries officials now insert bar code-like tags into the skulls of fish, instead of the bulky gill-plate tags they used to use. These tags stay with the fish and help biologists keep track of population dynamics via electronic technology.

Researchers at The University of Texas at Port Aransas have learned how to stimulate growth hormones in the ovaries of trout. And a team of Louisiana State University scientists has developed methods for preserving trout sperm so they can perfect trophy-targeted artificial insemination of the species.

These agencies might not be consciously working toward the creation of a super trout, but you can bet they see the potential of such an accomplishment. The speckled trout is quickly becoming to the saltwater community what the largemouth bass is to the freshwater industry, and this is creating a serious economic incentive to create bigger, better fish.

Do you think Texas bass fishing would be as popular without the introduction of the Florida strain largemouth? I think not. On the same note, creating more large trout would benefit everyone. How many Corkies do you think were sold after Jim Wallace broke the state record with one back in 1996? Get the picture?

The speckled trout is the largemouth bass of the Texas saltwater scene. It is the species that drives the fishing market and regulation principles, and has become a key component of TPWD hatchery production. I do not know if we will ever see a Lone Star Share-a-Sow-Speck program, but we are moving from ShareLunker to SuperSpeck at rapid pace, and technology, genetic research, and the ingenuity of fisheries biologists is leading the way.

The fact we are even discussing such matters shows we have come a very long way n both managing and fishing for speckled trout. It seems a lifetime ago that I caught my very first on a Zebco 404 fishing from the bank a few miles from home. Now when I have the opportunity to seek specks all along the Gulf Coast, I thank God for my first introductions to these amazing fish and for the fact hundreds of thousands of kids in coming generations will get the same opportunities.

I hope it puts a smile on their faces like it did me more than 30 years ago.

chapter one

Biology:
Speckled trout biology, myths, and angler's attitudes

Cynoscion nebulosis, the spotted seatrout or "speckled trout" is a fascinating species. This is especially true when examining the real story of the species life history. I say "real story" because "my grandpa told me" myth-information pervades the trout fishing community. Learning the truth about trout is like reading the book after seeing the movie. The facts about trout are far more interesting than the myths told and retold in bait shops.

LIFE HISTORY

According to Texas Parks & Wildlife Department (TPWD) data, the speckled trout occurs in the Western Atlantic and Gulf of Mexico, ranging from Massachusetts to the Yucatan peninsula. The fish is a member of the croaker family (*Sciaenidae*) and is first cousin to the Atlantic croaker, red drum, black drum, and sand seatrout.

According to a TPWD publication, *The Spotted Seatrout in Texas*:

Sexual maturity is reached at two years of age and eggs number from 100,000 in small fish to more than one million in large females. Spawning occurs inside the bays near grass beds where the newly hatched young find food and shelter. Recent findings show that fish spawn sometime between dusk and dawn. Spotted seatrout have a protracted spring and summer spawning period which peaks during May-July. Two-, three-, and four-year-old fish make up the bulk of the spawning population.

The growth rate of spotted seatrout differs between males and females, with females growing faster. Approximate lengths at various years of age are given in the following table.

AGE	MALE	FEMALE
1	9"	8"
2	14"	17"
3	17"	20"
4	18"	23"
5	18"	24"
6	19"	25"
7	19"	26"

Most large spotted seatrout caught are females and commonly live to be nine or 10 years of age. Anglers long ago recognized that very large trout were usually female and appropriately called them "sow" trout. The record trout taken by rod and reel in Texas measured 33 3/4" and weighed 13 pounds 9 ounces.

Chapter 1 | Biology

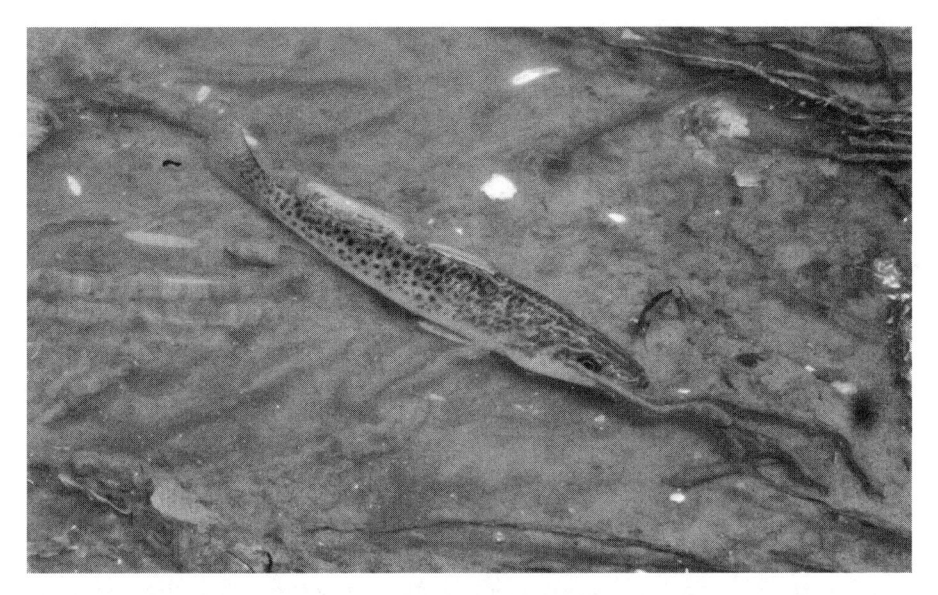

Speckled trout grow quickly and in areas where quality habitat allows them to be able to hide from predators at a young age survivability is strong.

The species is highly prolific and can stand incredible harvests from both recreational and commercial anglers. During the 1990s, the average trout harvest in Louisiana was 11.5 million fish. The last year I have complete data for was 1996, and the harvest was 11,136,756. On top of that, Louisiana had a commercial speckled trout fishery until March of 1997. During the 1990s, commercial take ranged from 650,000 pounds to more than 1.2 million pounds.

Combined commercial and recreational harvest killed a lot of trout in Louisiana, yet the species' astonishing resilience sustained the pressure and recreational fishing remained excellent. With the cessation of commercial harvest, the quality of fish improved. In May 1997, the Lake Calcasieu water body record was broken, and during the spring of 2002, three fish caught in Calcasieu and Lake Ponchatrain broke into the state's Top 10 list. The fishery is in the best condition it has ever been.

THE AMAZING SPECKLED TROUT SPAWN

Over the years, I found Louisiana State University (LSU) among the best in terms of speckled trout studies. We have already learned what TPWD has to say about the trout's life history. Now let's look at LSU's observations:

LSU researchers have done an incredible job of investigating the spawning potential of trout. They recently discovered females start spawning at 12 inches and males at 10 inches. That is in stark contrast to other findings, mostly by state fish and game departments. This will be examined more closely elsewhere in this book. Officials with the Louisiana Department of Wildlife and Fisheries recently changed regulations in the southwestern corner of the state knocking back the bag limit from 25 to 15 fish per angler, which according to guides is already helping the already amazing fishery.

Many anglers wonder why they sometimes catch all male trout (identifiable by their incessant croaking) in certain areas. As it turns out, male speckled trout will gather by the thousands to form what scientists call "drumming aggregations," making all kinds of racket underwater.

According to a report from Sea Grant, administered by the National Oceanographic and Atmospheric Administration (NOAA): "During spawning season, males form drumming aggregations, which can number in the hundreds or even thousands of fish. Within these aggregations each male vibrates his air bladder, producing a croaking sound. When combined with many other males' sounds, the result sounds like drumming or roaring.

"The sound attracts females ready to spawn. Both drumming aggregations and spawning take place in areas 6 to 165 feet deep with good tidal flow, such as passes and channels. Spawning begins at sunset and is usually over by midnight."

The report states that this spawning-related activity depends on environmental factors, such as currents, salinity, and temperature: "The two most important factors that determine when speckled trout spawn are water temperature and day length. Egg development begins to take place as days become longer in spring. Water temperatures of 68 degrees seem to trigger spawning, which continues as water temperature increases. Peak spawning takes place between 77 and 86 degrees. The cycle of the moon also seems to affect spawning, with spawning peaks occurring on or near the full moons of the spring and summer months. Females may spawn every seven to 14 days during the April to September spawning period."

Speaking of spawning, 1038 speckled trout, ranging in age from one to five years, were collected in a study by researchers in South Carolina to determine spawning potential, according to *Lagniappe*, the research publication of Louisiana State University (LSU).

Spawning potential is crucial in terms of trout management, as size and bag limits are generally based on this principle. From the LSU report: "The smallest mature female was 9.8 inches long. By 10.6 inches, 50 percent of females were mature. At 11.9 inches, 100 percent of the females are mature in South Carolina (compared to 10.6 inches in Louisiana). The researchers found that females became mature about one full year after their birth. While, not all age one females are mature on their birthday, they can be expected to become mature before the spawning season ended."

Researchers found that trout at age one spawn once every 4.7 days; age two fish, every 4.2 days; and age three fish, every 4.0 days.

"This is quite close to what has been found for Gulf States trout. As to how many eggs were laid per spawn, the estimates were 145,452 eggs for age 1 fish; 291,123 for age-2 fish; and 529,976 for age-3 fish. This is higher than the latest research indicates for Louisiana specks."

Interestingly, researchers reported that as the spawning season progressed, the size of the eggs laid by each female grew steadily smaller: "This had been noted before by other scientists, and has produced quite a bit of speculation as to why it occurs. One researcher suggested that the eggs didn't need to be as large nearer the end of the spawning season as near the beginning because more food was available in the water later for the newly hatched larval fish."

The report said others theorized some sort of relationship based on water temperature existed, with the higher the water temperature, the smaller the egg produced by the female: "Another suggestion was that as the spawning season wore on, females become leaner and less plump, therefore producing smaller eggs. Indeed, in this study, the females did become less plump later and later in the season."

The final tally was that, annually, age one fish produced 3.2 million eggs per year; age two, 9.5 million; age three, 17.6 million; age four, 24.4 million; and age five, 31.6 million.

"From these figures, it would seem almost a [surety] that the oldest fish produce a much higher percentage of the annual spawn than the younger fish. However, in this study, over half the fish were one-year-olds. There were twice as many one-year-olds as two-year-old fish, and seven times more than three-year-olds. As a result, age one fish produced 29 percent of the total spawned eggs; age two produced 39 percent; age three, 21 percent; age four, 7 percent; and age 5, only 7 percent of total spawn."

FEEDING AND THROWING UP, YES THROWING UP

The regional management plan of the Gulf States Marine Fisheries Commission (GSMFC) sheds light on an often-misunderstood part of speckled trout behavior: feeding. It shows that one researcher examined stomach volumes and concluded that spotted seatrout fed more heavily in early to mid morning.

Chapter 1 | Biology

The author holds in his hand a three-inch speckled trout being stocked into the Sabine Lake system. He felt like a proud Papa as he caught many of the broodstock that were bred to produce these fingerlings. Due to the hard work of Moore, Captains Skip James and Phillip Samuels along with the Golden Triangle CCA Chapter, Sea Center Texas was able to stock 1.5 million trout fingerlings in the area during 2008. The Sea Center crew works hard to stock key areas along the Upper Coast.

According to GSMFC: "He also noted that while feeding spotted seatrout appeared to regurgitate portions of food, which floated to the surface and created an oil slick. This phenomenon would explain why fishermen often look for "slicks" when attempting to locate feeding and schooling spotted seatrout."

GSMFC also noted that another researcher, "observed that record shrimp harvests were occurring during their food habits study; however, spotted seatrout were not utilizing them to any great extent. Although shrimp, were present, Miles (1951) found that mullet were the preferred food for spotted seatrout."

Much of the research out there sheds light on why anglers catch relatively few huge speckled trout. A big part of it is rarity, but otherwise, anglers by and large are not fishing in the right spots or using the right bait.

According to Sea Grant Louisiana's Jerald Host: "Aside from the fact that there are many more small trout than large ones, large speckled trout are very specialized creatures. Large trout are not as widely distributed as small trout. The largest trout are taken in the spring, next largest in winter, then fall and summer, out in the Gulf.

"Large but lesser sized trout are taken near beaches, lesser still in lakes and bays, and the smallest usually in the marsh. Anglers prefer to fish for specks in summer and the second preference is fall. Fishing is most intense in sheltered inside waters. More big trout are caught in spring because they move into shallow beach and bay habitats at that time for their first spawn of the season. The rest of the summer and early fall, the larger trout tend to stay in cooler Gulf waters and only periodically enter beach and bay habitats for subsequent spawns.

"Many of the large fish winter offshore, with a few wintering in the interior marshes, where they are very sluggish. Large trout also have very different food habits than school trout. Small trout eat large

Chapter 1 | Biology

Some anglers like the author pictured here just like to catch fish. If it is a monster, that's great, but if not, the joy of being outdoors is still there.

amounts of shrimp and other crustaceans. As trout become larger, their diet shifts toward fish, the larger, the better. Studies in Texas and Mississippi show that really big trout strongly prefer to feed on mullet; a large trout will find the largest mullet it can handle and try to swallow it. Often the mullet is half or two-thirds as large as the trout. The key to catching large trout is to fish where they are and use big baits."

Migration is perhaps the most mysterious and often debated aspect of speckled trout. Some anglers believe that during winter, all of the trout leave the bays and go into the Gulf. Others say they congregate in the mouths of rivers.

Dispelling Myths

MYTH NO. 1: Trout are highly migratory.

According to TPWD, speckled trout spend most of their lives within five miles of where they were born. Nearly 90 percent of all fish recovered in a tagging program came from the same bay in which they were tagged. While many trout move into deeper water during cold weather, there is no scientific evidence of a winter migration to the Gulf. Research shows that some fish may move to the Gulf to escape blowing northers, but this is temporary and the fish return once weather abates.

A study by the Gulf States Marine Fisheries Commission (GSMFC) report shows that one researcher tagged more than 2600 trout and received 50 returns. Of these, 20 came from the release point. Similar findings were reported by researcher Rogillio with 98 percent of the returns coming within 1.5 kilometers of the release point, while another noted that two spotted seatrout tagged in Calcasieu Lake were recaptured over 160 kilometers away east in Atchafalaya Bay, Louisiana.

The report details that in Texas, of 20,912 tagged trout released in Texas marine waters, 1367 were recaptured. About 84 percent were caught in the same bay where released; eight percent were caught in another bay; and five were recaptured in the Gulf. Of 588 spotted seatrout tagged in the Gulf surf, 14 were recaptured, 12 in the Gulf and two in Texas bays. The greatest distance traveled by any Texas spotted seatrout released in the Gulf was 106 kilometers, and in the bay it was 219.

This lack of major migration has created genetic isolation in some trout populations, which is why Texas Parks & Wildlife Department officials will stock trout fingerlings only in waters from which their parents were caught.

MYTH NO. 2: Trout never eat crabs.

A study conducted in Louisiana analyzed the stomach contents of 368 speckled trout caught in marshes. A total of 52 were empty. Baitfishes were present in 74.4-percent of stomachs, and crustaceans (crabs and shrimp) in 25.3-percent. In this same period, forage base samples showed crustaceans had become more prevalent.

Quality trout like this one caught by Capt. Bruce Miller are not the product of chance. They are the result of a deep conservation ethic that is powerful along the Texas Coast.

Saltwater Strategies Book Series: **TEXAS TROUT TACTICS**

One of the reasons speckled trout are susceptible to winter freezes like the catastrophic ones in 1983 and 1989 is because they do stay in bay systems in the winter.

MYTH NO. 3: Specks are related to rainbow trout.

Speckled trout are in the same family as croaker. You may have heard trout make a croaking noise—now you know why. It is a genetic thing. They are in no way kin to the freshwater rainbow trout.

MYTH NO. 4: Trout spawn in brackish water.

Speckled trout spawn mostly in the early evening in parts of the bay with the highest salinity. Contrary to popular belief, they usually do not move into streams or river mouths to spawn. Developing eggs are at the mercy of tidal and wind-driven currents, but develop rapidly. The larval trout hatches about 12 to 20 hours after spawning and can swim on their own another day or two later.

MYTH NO. 5: Male trout outlive females.

Female trout outlive males. Males may live six years, whereas females can live up to 10 years. By age two or three, both males and females have are about a foot in length, and natural mortality during these prime year is about 50 percent.

ANGLER OPINIONS

Speckled trout are major players in Texas saltwater fishing. No other species comes close to drawing as much attention from recreational anglers, and hence outdoor media and biologists. Speckled trout are genuine saltwater superstars. According to a study conducted by Robert B. Ditton and Don Clark of Texas A & M University, speckled trout command super dollars. In the 1992-1993 license year, for example, Texas anglers spent $495 million seeking specks.

The wild thing about that number is it does not include rods, reels, lures, wading belts, or boats. The figure represents only fuel, hotel, meals, ice, and bait costs; there are millions more unaccounted speckled trout dollars out there.

The study also indicates anglers spent $132 on a typical spotted seatrout fishing trip.

The average trip lasted two days and involved one-way travel of 85 miles. Anglers surveyed spent an average of 27 days fishing per year, with an average 18.9 days in saltwater. Nearly all saltwater fishing was for trout. This survey covered more than economics and uncovered some interesting facts about angler attitudes toward speckled trout management.

Most anglers surveyed disagreed with the statement: "Recreational anglers were putting too much fishing pressure on speckled trout populations." About one percent participated in saltwater fishing tournaments. Of those who reported fishing in tournaments, most reported fishing in only one or two tournaments in the previous 12 months. Anglers were split on whether saltwater tournaments were putting too much pressure on spotted seatrout populations. Thirty-two percent agreed, 31 percent disagreed, and 37 percent were neutral. Most anglers expressed support for a requirement that tournaments have a permit from TPWD. Even more felt tournaments should return a percentage of their purses to TPWD to support saltwater fisheries management.

About 42 percent of anglers were opposed to designating certain areas as catch-and-release-only for spotted seatrout. An option which would allow anglers to keep one trophy fish while fishing in catch and release areas, did not decrease opposition. Opposition further increased to 57 percent when anglers were asked about having their favorite fishing area designated as catch-and-release-only.

Most anglers supported a regulation that would allow them to keep one fish under the 15" limit with the current bag limit of 10 fish, but fewer supported the idea of being allowed to keep two fish under the limit. Fifty percent supported lowering the minimum length from 15 to 14 inches and keeping the current bag limit.

Responses became more interesting regarding questions about trophy trout management. Roughly 23 percent felt there was too much fishing pressure on trophy-sized trout, and 28 percent supported a requiring that all trophy-sized trout be released—provided that one trophy fish per day could be retained. Nearly half supported a limit on the number of trophy spotted seatrout an angler could keep per year. Sixty-one percent would support a trophy tag available at no charge when they purchased a license. Seventy percent of anglers were opposed to a trophy tag if it was at additional cost. Opposition decreased to 44 percent if revenue from tag sales went only for trout management. If limited to one trophy tag per year, 45 percent were opposed. If multiple tags could be purchased throughout the year, 5 percent were opposed.

When anglers were asked if they would purchase the tag at varying prices from $5 to $50 rather than release all spotted seatrout over 28 inches, 83 percent would not purchase the tag. For those willing to pay for a trophy tag for spotted seatrout, the average maximum agreeable price was $8. The most commonly cited reasons for valuing the tag at zero dollars were "I cannot afford any greater cost of fishing" and "I feel I should be able to keep any size speckled trout at no extra cost."

As noted earlier, this survey was conducted several years ago. A similar study is underway now that will dig even deeper into the attitudes and economics of coastal fishermen. I would be willing to bet good money the new study will show those speckled trout anglers are spending more money and have more conservative attitudes now than they did 10 years ago.

The question is: How do we sustain that resource under increasing pressure from anglers, industry, and the ever-present threat red tide outbreak or catastrophic freeze like we had in 1983? This issue will grow in scope as speckled trout continue to steal the saltwater spotlight.

chapter two

Seasonal Patterns:
The best times and tactics for the seasons

SPRING

It has been popular belief for many years that trout migrate from the Gulf of Mexico into bay systems during the early part of spring. Research conducted by the Texas Parks & Wildlife Department (TPWD) and other agencies show there is little migration of the species. Trout tend to stay within a few miles of where they are born. Some trout will come in and out of the Gulf at the southern end of a bay on big tides, and some trout seek sanctuary in the deep water of ship channels during winter, but for the most part, trout that live in the bay stay there year-round.

Research conducted by the Texas Parks & Wildlife Department (TPWD) shows trout exhibit territorial behavior. One study indicates speckled trout spend most of their lives within a five-mile radius of the spawning site.

Capt. Mike Denman caught this big trout on a black Mirrolure fished on a muddy bottom during the month of February. Winter is a great time to catch big trout, especially on muddy bottoms on warm afternoons. The black mud draws in heat and increases the surrounding water temperature thus drawing in baitfish and predators alike.

Nearly 90-percent of all fish recovered from a tagging program instituted several years ago were caught in the same bay officials tagged them. While many trout move into deeper waters during wintertime, there is no scientific data to back the assertion that most trout migrate to the Gulf during winter. Research shows that some fish may move to the Gulf to escape blowing "northers", but this migration may only last a few days. Most of the trout are hiding out in the deep water of ship channels and other canals.

This isolation of speckled trout populations is so dramatic it affects their genetics. For example, TPWD has learned trout from one bay system cannot be stocked in another because of genetic differences due to population isolation. A trout caught in the Chandeleur Islands could not be successfully stocked in Baffin Bay. The Galveston Bay complex is known to have at least two separate genetic strains. Those caught in Trinity Bay are different than those caught in West Galveston Bay. Our eyes may not pick up these differences, but they go a long way to illustrate the fallacy of the notion of a large-scale trout migration.

Chapter 2 | Seasonal Patterns

Capt. Bruce Shuler, pictured here, believes wadefishing is the most productive way to approach super-sized trout which can be easily spooked and elusive.

Redfish, on the other hand, which are known to be highly migratory, can be caught and stocked anywhere along the Gulf coast. A redfish caught in East Galveston Bay could be stocked in Alabama's Mobile Bay. Reds are migratory, trout are not.

This should dispel some of the myths about spring trout fishing. Now, on to where and when to catch the fish.

When winter loosens its grip, anglers can find the largest trout in and around the passes and shorelines near the Gulf of Mexico. Baitfishes can be scarce this time of year, and the passes offer a constant influx of various forage species. Top areas include the King Ranch shoreline in South Texas, Galveston's Rollover and San Luis passes, and any number of spots in Laguna Madre.

Wade-fishing along the south shoreline of a bay continues to be productive into late spring. Look for concentrations of mullet to attract the trout this time of year. The concentrations do not have to be huge. Good numbers of trout can be found under relatively small schools of mullet

In recent years, I detailed the benefits of fishing with soft plastic jerkbaits during spring. I have tremendous success fishing with them around shell and mud when other lures simply would not deliver. Reports from East Galveston Bay in the spring of 2001 showed that soft plastic jerkbaits like Bass Assassins were responsible for catching the majority of the fish. That spring, by the way, was a very, very slow one. Jerkbaits delivered the goods.

In that same year, Matagorda Bay guide Tommy Countz reported the same thing: Good numbers of specks on pearl/chartreuse Norton Sand Eel Jr's worked over scattered shell in East Bay when the brutal winds of spring laid.

The Hackberry Rod & Gun Club, which has probably been responsible for putting more anglers on trout than any other similar organization, has been using jerkbaits for years with great success. Lake Calcasieu reports usually detail good catches on lures like Slimy Slugs fished over shell.

Savvy anglers know it is important to "match the hatch"—use lures that mimic what the game fish are preying on—and this time of year it is sand eels. It could also be marine worms, which are common periodically along the coast. Again, it is all about "matching the hatch." That is exactly what soft plastic jerkbaits do. They imitate the late winter/early spring prey items of speckled trout and give anglers a chance to catch fish during one of the most challenging periods of the year.

Look for deep oyster reefs to provide some of the best trout fishing during spring. Oyster reefs are loaded with sand eels and other baitfishes when other parts of a bay have very little bait. Additionally, these deeper oyster reefs hold more saltwater than do shallow areas. The saltiest water hangs on the bottom. This is a major drawing card at a time when bay systems are often diluted with freshwater runoff. Speckled trout love structure. The vast oyster reefs that cover large sections of bays provide structure. Anglers wanting to score on serious numbers of speckled trout should consider fishing oyster reefs.

The general practice while fishing reefs is to make long drifts with the current. A good tip is to use a drift sock to slow down boat movement. A slower drift will make for less hang-ups and greater bite detection.

Sounds simple enough, doesn't it? The reality is that understanding and fishing around oyster reefs can be complicated. An angler has to consider everything from depth, tidal movement and predator-prey relations to water clarity and the all-important influx of freshwater. Yes, oyster reefs can be one of the best places to cash in on consistent speckled trout fishing action, but you've got to learn how to properly mine the shell to harvest the big rewards.

A drift sock will slow down your drift during strong tidal movements and allow you to more effectively cover oyster reefs and other structure.

Eel imitation lures are a surefire way to catch trout in the spring. Sand eels are one of the most prolific prey items this time of year, especially around oyster reefs.

Let's look at flooding again.

Bay systems are prone to flooding in the spring. The flooding can get so bad that surface water miles out into the Gulf of Mexico can be almost purely fresh. Where do the speckled trout go during these floods? Do they move miles into the Gulf of Mexico to seek refuge? Some of them probably do, but the reality is that many (probably most) speckled trout concentrate in the deep water of bay systems. Saltwater is heavier than freshwater so it goes to the bottom and that's where the trout will be. The deepest water will be the saltiest water, and on ecosystems like the Galveston Bay and Sabine Lake, many of the oyster reefs are in deep water. The reefs on the southern end of the bays are especially good places to look for speckled trout because they have a strong tidal flow, which can bring in saltier water from the Gulf. During spring floods, oyster reefs covered by deep water can be virtually covered with speckled trout.

"We've seen situations on the Upper Coast where spring floods in the bay, in combination with low oxygen levels in the Gulf, pushed speckled trout onto oyster reefs and it put an immense amount of pressure on the fish," said Texas Parks & Wildlife Department biologist Jerry Mambretti. "The fish were virtually trapped and were fairly easy pickings. Our dockside surveys revealed a high level of harvest at these times."

All oyster reefs are not created equal and all parts of an oyster reef are not the same. It is important to look for structure within the structure. An oyster reef is a structure all by itself, but there is structure on top of that structure. A big clump of oysters rising up on a slight ridge on a reef with an average depth of 10 feet is structure on structure. A sunken boat on a reef is structure on structure.

I once read an article that said walleye in the Great Lakes use big clumps of mussel and wrecks to "push off" and give extra propulsion toward a baitfish. This could be why trout and other predatory bay fish are so bonded to structure during spring. Since they have slow metabolisms, any boost to their speed can be a big help in catching prey. It is just a theory.

Galveston Guide Capt. Jim Leavelle said drop-offs are also important things to look for on an oyster reef. "Drop-offs are very important to keep a lookout for. A ledge that drops off to 16 feet on a 10 foot deep reef is a must-fish spot. These are the kind of places speckled trout will gang up to intercept baitfish."

Leavelle advised letting out extra line out over these spots to make sure baits reach the fish: "If you just jump over these spots without letting some extra line out, you may not reach the fish. Keep your electronics on and look for the drop-off. When you hit it, let out some extra line and you'll probably catch some fish. It is not sure-fire, but it is awfully close."

An indispensable tool in reef fishing is a marker buoy. You can purchase these or make your own out of two-liter cola bottles. When coming across a hotspot, throw out the buoys so you can return. There might be 200 fish bunched up in a 20-yard spot, and that might be where they stay all day. You have to stay within the bite window to be successful.

You must pay attention to details. There are plenty of reefs to mine and, while you may not strike gold, the glisten of silver scales with black spots is enough to appease most anglers. That includes me.

SUMMER

Summer offers some of the fastest-paced action of the year. Big trout can be caught everywhere from the surf to the upper ends of bay systems, and this is when they get into a predictable bite pattern. Summer is indeed a good time to be an angler in search of trout on the Gulf coast.

Let's start with big fish first, since seeking them is a little different than looking for frying pan-sized fish. These brutes aren't as easy to catch as schoolies, but they are out there for the angler who knows where to look and does not mind taking "extreme" measures.

Sabine Lake guide Capt. Skip James said one of his favorite ways to catch summer trophy trout is to target them among smaller schooling trout and redfish: "For a guy looking to bag some big trout, look to the outside of trout schools. What I am about to say has been highly controversial because it sounds so unscientific, but it is well documented. Anyone who watches Discovery Channel enough can tell you that fish feed in distinct phases. I think redfish are some of the easiest to pattern in this regard."

James says that schooling activity is best in the mid-bay area on most systems. On Lake Sabine, James launches at the causeway, runs four to five miles due north early in the morning, and looks for tell-tale signs of schooling. He said if you do not see any birds, look for the less obvious signals: "Game fish feed in four distinct phases: packing, corralling, ambush and mop-up. Packing involves the fish coming together to terrorize the baitfish. This usually happens early on. It's during the next phase, corralling, that we start to notice some action, like nervous pogey-menhaden, scurrying shrimp, and jumping ladyfish.

"During the ambush period, the feeding reaches a feverish frenzy as the fish turn from passive to highly aggressive. This is the phase that the birds work and it is when you want to have your bait in the water.

"To catch big trout around the schools, I recommend a Rat-L-Trap or a big, heavy spoon. Use something that you can chunk out there and reach the fish with, plus it can get down toward the bottom fast. Additionally, have a few extra guns ready to shoot with. If you catch the fish on the feed, do not bother to unhook if you're legal. Just lay it down for a second and fire another shot. Its important to maximize your time during the feeding frenzy."

James said that when targeting big trout, it is crucial to avoid the small ones. He recommended backing off of a school if you catch a couple of small trout. They will get your bait before the big ones can, so leave them be. Not one to look a gift horse in the mouth, James sticks around if the trout have any size to them, but staying on the smaller ones is a no-no: "If I go in and catch a couple of really little trout right off of the bat, I circle where I think the school is and try to find the bigger ones. Often they will be on the outer edges of the trout, but you may have to search a little to find them."

The final stage of feeding is mop-up. This occurs after the main feeding is over and the fish seemingly get lockjaw. This is a great time to move in on an area where trout have been schooling to find the reds. James said that, more often than not, they will move in on the remnants of a baitfish school and start biting when the trout leave: "When the main bite is over, I will switch over from a Rat-L-Trap or spoon to a shrimp tail or Cocahoe Minnow and bounce it along the bottom, trying to rattle any roving reds' attention. Glow and chartreuse are the best colors."

James believes a common mistake is to leave an area during the mop-up period. The best bet is to set the trolling motor on low and

The late Capt. Daniel Pyle taught the author a lot about catching big trout.

cruise the perimeter, making 45-degree fan casts so that you cover every angle. Think of redfish as scavengers waiting to attack the remnants of the trout's prey.

Another common error is leaving when the sun gets high. Early morning is usually best, but on the murkier waters near the Sabine and Neches Rivers and at Sabine Pass, sunlight penetrating into the deeper water often stimulates more feeding, according to James: "This is a method I've worked really hard at using on Sabine, but it can apply to any coastal bay system. There are lots of big trout in Texas waters, and anglers who do not mind thinking of their fishing in such a scientific way can utilize it to great success."

Another option for anglers looking to score on trout during summer is at the nearshore oil platforms (short rigs). I go into extreme detail on short rig fishing in another chapter, but I want to emphasize these areas are tremendous for trout in summer. The same goes for jetties.

An entire chapter of this book is dedicated to the intricacies of jetty fishing, so details will be spared here. It is worth noting that jetties are among the better spots to locate good numbers of trout in summer months. One complaint I have heard from several anglers is they are afraid to fish in their flat-bottomed aluminum boats at the jetties. The only boat I own is a flat-bottomed aluminum boat, and we do just fine. An angler simply needs to go on calm days and be careful running the ship channel.

Port O'Connor guide Capt. Cody Adams said gas wells are some of his favorite spots to locate summer trout. "There are about 20 gas wells in Espiritu Santo Bay that I fish. The best way to fish them is to target the shell pads at the bottom. Bouncing a soft plastic will often draw a strike, but fishing with live croakers can be unbelievable. Croaker fishing is very consistent. The gas wells are a good backup plan when you want to go exploring."

Gas wells offer structure, which is something trout are very fond of. Structure does not have to be mammoth. The shell pads from abandoned wells are tremendous, and anglers who have their GPS numbers tend to find fish when no one else can.

Chris Kent of Crème Lures caught this nice trout while fishing with the author during the heat of the day when most anglers went home. They were actually searching for schooling redfish but found some large trout they just could not pass up.

Another exciting summer option noted by Adams is running the surf. He fishes out of Pass Cavalo. When light southeast winds blow, the fishing is tough to beat and much of this has to do with structure along the beach. The only structure on most beaches is sand and more sand. In this area, however, there are a number of shrimp boat wrecks that always hold fish in summer.

"Throwing live croaker around those wrecks can be downright scary. Those fish get in there thick. Artificials will also produce. A

51M MirrOlure or even a sinker like the 52 series will catch a bunch of trout. So will topwaters and silver spoons."

While silver spoons may be effective for trout, a gold spoon fished in the surf is a great way to bag a few bonus redfish. "There are a lot of reds in the surf, but people tend to forget about them when the trout fishing is good," continued Adams. "If you want to target reds, throw a gold spoon out there and you'll usually catch one. The only problem is that Spanish mackerel and jack crevalle are common. One will cut your line and the other will steal your line, so be prepared."

Wildlife photographer Gerald Burleigh caught this huge speck on a topwater plug fished in the marsh surrounding Sabine Lake during the spring. Topwaters imitate mullet which are the top prey item of trophy-sized specks.

Again, we will not go into great detail on surf fishing because it is covered elsewhere in far more detail. We will, however, cover ship channel fishing.

Ship channels seem unlikely places for speckled trout. Compared to the pristine setting of a marsh, ship channels seem polluted—and probably are. That does not mean anglers will not find trout. In fact, some of the very best fishing during summer comes from ship channel areas. Trout often seek cooler water during the peak heat of summer, and that is exactly what ship channels offer. Anglers should not just go out to a ship channel and start fishing. They should look for "transition zones." These are areas where the deep water meets a shallow flat.

Trout often hang in the deep water during periods of high tide and then move onto the flats to hunt for baitfish. Learning how to properly read a tide chart is very important in this regard.

When ship channels are dug, the "spoils" or shell and mud gathered from the bottom are often laid alongside the main channel. These areas create little havens for speckled trout. Find "spoils" in the months of July and August and you will find trout.

Ship channels are also known for night fishing. Many of the refinery docks along the Gulf coast have huge lights along the water, and this attracts trout by the thousands. Crappie fishermen in freshwater have known for years that lights attract baitfishes, which in turn attracts crappie. Ditto for speckled trout. If you are ever driving along a ship channel at night and see boats staked out around these docks, remember the location and go back there. They were probably catching lots of fish.

Summer is also great for fishing with "green lights," which have become standard issue along the Gulf Coast. These colored lights penetrate the water in a way that old-fashioned floating crappie lights never could, and they draw in trout like crazy. I have fished with green lights in ship channels, at jetties and on bay systems and had baitfishes gathered so thick it seemed I could walk on them. On several occasions, trout started gang-attacking baitfish and creating images reminiscent of schooling bonita feeding in the open Gulf of Mexico.

There are basically two different kinds of green lights on the market: floating and submersible. The submersible kind seems to work a little better than the floaters, but I have no complaints with mine. It has helped me to catch fish when nothing else would.

Fall

During that sort of strange transition period between summer and fall, I have found shorelines to be extremely productive for trout.

Actually they can be productive year-round but I chose to discuss fishing them in this section because this is an overlooked time of year and the big tides we get in late August and early September as summer is fading away push some of our biggest and best trout to the shorelines. Most anglers have little understanding of fishing shorelines for speckled trout.

I say this because I am one of those anglers seeking to improve my success and rehabilitate myself from going for the obvious and not focusing on the hidden ecosystems (and sow specks) that dwell shorelines along the Gulf Coast. Along the northern coastline in Texas and throughout Louisiana in particular, speck fishing in bays from summer through fall has much to do with finding fish feeding under the birds and under huge schools of menhaden. The reason is this is pretty simple fishing. A pair of binoculars and an observant eye can have you on fast-paced fishing action in no time; however most of these fish are small.

Think about it. How many true trophy-sized specks have you ever caught under the birds or schooling on the main bay? Sure, there are a few out there, but the guys you see bringing in the big ones almost

Some of the best trout angling can be found in and around ship channels, especially at night.

never target fish on the main bay and are as tight-lipped as a CIA operative about their fishing holes. That's because most of the time, they are targeting shorelines that you motor past chasing little trout under the birds.

"It wasn't until I started doing a lot of hardcore wadefishing that I really saw the importance of fishing for the big trout along shorelines," said angler Phillip Samuels of Groves, TX.

Samuels said most anglers take their cues from obvious visual indicators, but should start looking at the slightly obscure.

"Big trout don't like to have to move around too much to feed. They are not nearly as aggressive or forceful as the smaller ones. Even when you are fishing under the birds, the bigger ones are always at the bottom below the little schoolies. Big trout get big because of several factors, one of them being they inhabit areas with a high concentration of food and a lower concentration of fishermen," Samuels said.

One such area along shorelines are stands of roseau cane, which has an intricate rooting system comparable to a miniature version of mangrove. On high tides, cane stands hold lots of baitfish, which hide from predators among the roots. Big trout will feed along the edges of this cane and quite often go untargeted.

"I've been known for catching flounder around roseau cane because it's a great ambush point for them. We do catch a lot of nice trout around these cane stands as well and it's for the same reasons. Big trout like an easy meal," said Capt. Skip James.

James also notes that when seeking big fish in these areas anglers should be mindful of making parallel casts along the shoreline, tight to the shore.

"On the low tides, especially in the fall, you can see there is some depth under the roots where the bait hides and the trout will sometimes feed right in there. Make sure and make parallel casts when you are wadefishing to cover ground. People tend to throw out from the shore and sometimes ignore what's really important: the shore itself."

James noted that even small differences in a bottom can be a huge factor in holding fish.

Trolling motors are an invaluable tool for anglers seeking trout. They allow them to maneuver quietly which is very, very important. Trout are spooky fish.

"Everyone knows shorelines with shell will hold some fish and the mouths of cuts will to. Sometimes though, just one small bowl formed by the current or perhaps a storm makes all the difference in the world in terms of holding fish," he said.

A fine case in point was my experience fishing Sabine Lake last year. Throughout 2006, I noticed that during high tides trout were holding super tight to the shorelines on the Louisiana shoreline. For much of the summer in particular, they were biting and the next day they have lockjaw or so I thought.

The pattern for much of the summer was there were gulls working over schools of trout all over the lake one day and then no gulls (or trout on the main lake) at all the next. While fishing with Mike Tennian of L&S Lures, I headed to the banks between Whisky Bayou and the Pines and found trout literally stacked against the shore. Most of the time trout are known for working out from the shorelines, but they were so tight to the bank that my partners and I were getting hits literally inches from the mud line. We were fishing with the Mirrolure Catch 5 and a variety of topwaters and caught the most fish by fishing them with a fast retrieve parallel to the shorelines. Most of the time you will cast toward the shore, but once we figured out the fish were literally hugging the bank, we took James' advice and switched to casting down the shoreline to maximize the fishing action.

The areas that held the most trout were where there was a concentration of shad mixed in with shrimp. We found lots of shad with minimal trout, but when there were some shrimp skipping the top of the water as well, the specks were present. The whole scenario had me scratching my head because my theory has been that trout prefer easy access over hard work and on the main body of the bay I could have swam like a fish and caught shad in my mouth. That is how thick they were. The next week I returned to do some wade fishing in that area and noticed something interesting about the bottom in this location. Over about 100-yard stretch between two well-defined points, the bottom dropped off steeply into some big potholes. I went from my waist deep to chest deep and then rose up to my knees. What I realized is that when Hurricane Rita blew through the area, it changed the bottom in this spot and made it deeper.

Then I got to looking at the cuts coming from the marsh. At the time, the tide was coming in strongly and was quite high which was the same situation that Tennian and I encountered before. I noticed there were a couple of small eddies in relation to the new ridges and potholes formed in the storm. The trout were feeding there because the shrimp and shad gathered in the eddy and at that point were probably trapped there by the feeding trout. This made perfect sense. That Louisiana shoreline tends to form eddies on tides on incoming tides around cuts, but they are usually small and filled with flounder. Because this location had several small cuts and major changes in topography, it formed a large eddy that is one giant pot of seafood gumbo for marauding specks.

In any bay system there can be dozens of spots like this that are ignored by most anglers.

"It has often been said that 10 percent of the fishermen catch 90 percent of the fish. A lot of it has to do with adherence to fishing little spots no one else targets and making note of every change in the bottom they see on a GPS or at least a good map. Attention to detail is everything from topography to timing," said trout specialist Capt. Shane Chesson.

Chesson said he and his guide partner Capt. Brian Fischer hit shorelines on East Galveston Bay early in the mornings and then back off later in the day during the summer.

"We like to start along the shore early working opening-morning-colored Saltwater Assassins and Skitter-Walks. We find that the trout like to hold to shorelines that are close to deeper water in the summer and as the day wears on, they will back off to deeper water," Chesson said

In terms of what kinds of shoreline to target, Chesson said he prefers those with mixed shell and with large concentrations of mullet.

"Mullet are very mobile and move around a lot but there are certain areas like around cuts in the marsh that hold lots of mullet and therefore usually hold some nice trout. When you start looking at these specific areas you will notice there are little washed out guts and humps and things formed by the current, which are perfect for giving trout a spot to ambush the mullet," he said.

As you can see, there is a lot more to shorelines than just a backdrop for your fishing adventures. If you're one of the anglers that already realize this, more power to you. However, if you like to spend a lot of times chasing smallish trout on the main body of the bay, then you might want to look at shorelines in a new light.

As soon as the big cold fronts start blowing through, the fishing gets less technical and far more fun. That is when the trout are biting under the birds.

The only technical part to fall fishing under the birds is to not run up on the birds (or the fish beneath them) with the big motor. Stop at least 50 yards away and use a trolling motor or the wind to move in close. Also, respect other anglers fishing the schools. It is highly disrespectful to fish right next to them. Fishing the same school is fine, but getting close enough to shake hands is rude and may earn you a good look at a middle finger—or maybe the whole fist.

These schooling trout will hit just about anything, including spoon, soft plastics, topwaters and lipless crankbaits.

Something I have noticed over the last few years is sometimes the trout want a really fast retrieve. And I do mean fast. Most anglers fishing soft plastics hop the bait up and down, but during the fall, sometimes the trout will hit only if you throw it out and reel it in as fast as possible. If you find a flock of birds obviously feeding on trout and cannot get the fish to hit, try this method. It usually works when nothing else does.

By nature, the biggest specimens of speckled trout are lazy. They are old, fat, and seem to have lost their vigor for fighting the young ones for shrimp and menhaden. That means when you run into a school of specks feeding in the fall, the biggest specks will be belly-to-the-bottom. Instead of fishing a soft plastic lure on a 1/8- or 1/4-ounce jighead, simply upgrade the head 1/2-ounce so it sinks to the bottom quickly. I personally prefer fishing with a 1/2-ounce silver spoon or deep-diving crankbait like the Fat Free Shad. I have started catching good numbers of trout on the Shad, which most anglers use for largemouth bass. It and other deep divers work for trout and are great for getting past the smaller surface feeders. Another way to get bigger trout as well as reds is to fish on the outside of the feeding frenzy. If I have had my fill of smallish trout or are simply hungry for some tasty redfish fillets, I pull up about 20 yards farther out than you would while trout fishing under the birds, and then make pattern casts around the school with a Rat-L-Trap or a 1/2-ounce gold Scent-Killer spoon. This spoon, manufactured right here in Texas, has a strip to hold scent, and is great for redfish. If you can't find this one, use whatever spoon you have. Live baiters can score by free-lining live finger mullet or small blue crab on a circle or Kahle hook. Anglers rarely use live crab in Texas waters, but it is very popular in Florida and it works here, too. Fiddler crabs will also work wonders, but they are very difficult to catch and I do not know of any bait camps that carry them.

During fall, wade-fishing also comes into play. Capt. Guy Schultz, who works in the Galveston system, said looking for cuts pouring out of marshy areas is one of the most proven producing methods: "The fall feeding pattern is based around the exodus of baitfish. They're leaving the marshes and the trout are following them. During the early part of the fall, look for fish to be around the cuts. As a few cold fronts make their way through, look to the main body of bay systems to find fish. They'll be feeding under flocks of seagulls."

WINTER

Enterprising anglers interested in catching trophy-sized speckled trout typically don waders and stalk specks in the shallows. Ideally you look for warm afternoons when the skies are clear.

Shallow areas with muddy

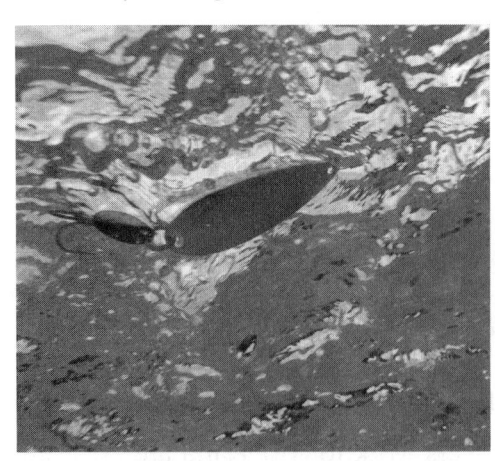

Spoons are easy to throw long distances, sink past the small fish quickly and are highly effective for speckled trout.

bottoms are one of the best areas to find trout during winter. The reason: on calm, clear days the dark-colored mud absorbs heat and warms the surround water a few degrees. This is highly appealing to baitfishes and the trout that pursue them.

If you decide to fish for big trout, fish slowly. A slow-sinking bait like a Corky Fat Boy or Mirrolure Catch 2000 is a top choice, but topwaters worked a little slower than usual can be productive. I like to fish topwater plugs year-round. Sometimes, in later winter and early spring, bay waters on bays will get murky and topwaters are easier for trout to locate.

Galveston-area guide George Knighten sometimes fishes Sabine, and is known as a wade-fishing specialist. He said using topwaters in murky water can be the ticket: "In the late winter and early spring, we get a lot of murky water in the Galveston bay system. I will often go to a very loud topwater plug to catch trout under these conditions. They can't really see very well when the water looks bad, but they can hear a topwater plug and many times that's enough to get them to hit."

While wade-fishing the Chandeleur Islands when water conditions were poor, topwaters were the go-to bait. At the time, the trout were feeding heavily on mullet, and I guess the sound of an injured mullet was what they wanted to hear. Since then, I've experienced the same thing on Sabine and in East Matagorda Bay.

DOA Baits owner Mark Nichols has a theory about fishing in winter that covers not only topwaters, but all styles of fishing. He says "Fish slower than evolution." That is not bad advice.

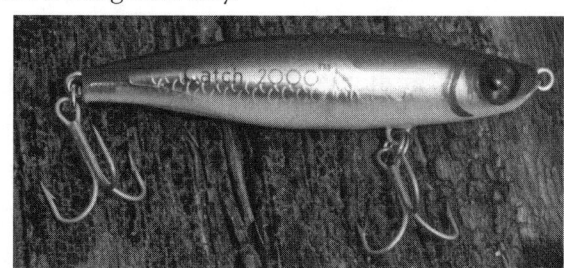

Slow-sinking lures like this Catch 2000 appeal to the super slow metabolism of specks in the winter. (Photo by Chester Moore, Jr.)

It is very important to focus on finding mullet in the winter. My biggest trout ever was caught in a channel in the marsh, where I spied a handful of mullet milling around—and it was not as if this area was alive with bait. The water was clear and I saw some mullet slowly trading between the channel and the shallower shoreline, and figured that was a good place to start. Two casts later, I was fighting the trout of a lifetime.

Mullet are an excellent indicator of how fish are behaving in winter and early spring. Most baitfishes are very small. Menhaden are miniscule, and you never see sand eels unless you are cleaning a fish full of them. Mullet, however, provide glimpses into what the water temperature is doing to the fish. They swim near the surface and will often lay in the shallows, presumably kick-starting their metabolism during warm spells.

I have learned to work lures to imitate the mullet I am seeing. If they are super sluggish and just kind of there, I go with a slow-sinker like the Chatter Tube or Catch 2000. I might even go to a chugging topwater plug like a Chug Bug. Chuggers are not very popular this time of year, but I think they are greatly overlooked. They allow you to fish slowly and closely mimic the action of slow moving mullet on the surface. Just gently chug the bait and then let it sit for a bit. Yes, this is about as exciting as watching paint dry, but when you get a blowup, you tend to forget about the boring routine. Funny, how that works.

If the mullet are more active—typically in February and early March on warm afternoons as the sun heats shallow mud flats—I go to a walking plug. I have had good luck with the Top Dog, Super Spook, and a host of others, but my favorite is the Skitter Walk. It is an easy-to-walk plug that effectively imitates the herky-jerky movements of a wounded mullet.

For those who prefer fishing with live bait, yes, live mullet can be effective this time of year. Fished on a free line and dragged slowly, almost as if fishing for flounder, it can be highly effective. It is also good for drifting over mud flats when the tides are high enough to allow fishing.

Probably the most important thing to remember is that trout might not be super-aggressive. You might simply feel tension on your line, not a big tug. This is even true for slow sinkers. Sometimes, you will just feel a slight "tick" that ends up being a beastly trout. Then again, this month they might brutalize your lures. It all depends on the weather, and as we know, March is a mixed bag on the Texas coast.

The author loves to fish mullet imitators like this Top Dog in the winter and early spring period. Here he shows off a monster speck caught in Aransas Bay.

Focus on the mullet and your bag might very well include the trout of a lifetime.

A few years ago, an angler told me he was catching big speckled trout in the marshes on the Louisiana side of Sabine Lake by looking for garfish. At first, I thought he was off in la-la land, and then I got to thinking that during February and early March, some of the best trout holes in that area have lots of gar in them. This got me to doing some calling around and poking around in these areas.

What I found out is there seems to be some sort of relationship between the gar and trout in these areas. Because they are simply wintering in the same waters, or the big trout are feeding on the gar's scraps. Weirder things have happened.

"In some of the areas we fish, the water really clears up in February and we see a lot of big alligator garfish just sort of slowly cruising around these canals, or sitting motionless on the bottom," said Capt. Skip James. "And quite a bit we have seen big trout right in there with the gar. It's kind of strange, but something we have seen more than a few times."

A few years ago, I got my first glimpse of this in a cut we call the "Dredge Hole." There were quite a few gar in the cut, and in a spot where I could see down a couple of feet was a 4-foot long gar with a big speck (probably in the 25- to 27-inch class) lying right next to it.

Of course, I had the bright idea that it would be really cool to bounce a lure off the side of the gar and catch the trout—sort of a billiards bank shot. The gar sped away and the trout disappeared in a cloud of silt kicked up by its armored companion. I did catch a couple of nice fish in that area that day, but none bounced off a gar.

This month, I will be attempting to catch some big specks, and when I fish those waters, I will be looking for garfish to lead me to the trout.

It is important to remember cold weather chills the metabolism of many freshwater and bay-dwelling fish, and certain pelagic species migrate to warmer areas. Nonetheless, there is good fishing to be found along the Gulf coast during winter months.

Finding big concentrations of speckled trout is tough this time of year. Fish are cold-blooded and do not really like winter. In fact, if they can find sanctuary from winter weather, they tend to do so, which is why warm water outfall canals are such great fishing holes. Along the Gulf coast there are several warm water discharges from energy plants and refineries that can harbor incredible numbers of fish—and quite often, the best bay fishing winter has to offer.

Chapter 2 | Seasonal Patterns

I grew up fishing around the Entergy Plant near Bridge City, Texas. It is like most outfits along the Texas coast in that it cools its turbines by pumping water from one canal and expelling it into another. In this case, the water is coming from a marsh bordering the Lower Neches Wildlife Management Area, and is exiting into a canal that leads to the mouth of the Neches River. Both usually hold salty water during winter.

Baitfishes congregate in such warm waters during cold spells, making the area a sort of buffet for a host of large predators like redfish and speckled trout. They're great for human predators too, since the cold-blooded fish become much more active feeders in these spots than in colder surrounding waters.

Warm-water discharges come in many forms. They can be a huge cooling plant that spews out thousands of gallons of warm water a minute, or a small drainage pipe or culvert that has a very light flow. Many times, chemical refineries will have small pump stations that produce warm water flow that diverts into underwater pipes. Any of these areas can hold a surprising amount of fish, but it is safe to say the more flow and the warmer the water compared to surrounding water, the more fish there will be.

An interesting phenomenon in these areas is that different species favor various degrees of warmth or current. For example, speckled trout are often found right next to the outflow pipes and prefer the areas where the water is warmest, but other species may act differently.

Something to keep in mind is that even small flows from a single drainpipe can draw fish. They may not hold massive schools of fish for long periods of time, but even a slight change for the positive in water temperature can make a difference in cold weather. It is very important to look for the little things in these spots, since very often that's all it takes to attract game fish.

An outfall canal on the Sabine River no longer pumps hot water, but fish still congregate there like it did. Old timers in the area say the fish in the area are genetically programmed to go there. Maybe so.

I've been a fan of fishing warm-water discharges for a long time, and have had numerous memorable outings on days when the "intelligent" thing to do was to stay home where it is warm. Actually, if catching fish makes you happy and the lack of consistent winter action is bugging you, it might be wise to check out some of the warm water discharges in your neck of the woods. They usually hold lots of fish, and that can be hard to find this time of year.

Remember, fish are often concentrated in such great numbers in these canals that they become easy pickings. Capt. Guy Schultz said the Houston Light and Power (HL&P) outfall in Trinity Bay is one such spot: "Everyone in our area has heard the stories of guys filling up boats full of fish in that area before limits were put in place, and I do not doubt those stories have a lot of truth to them. Sometimes catching fish in these areas is like shooting them in a barrel. It is up to the angler to abide by limits and do the right thing."

I agree with that statement 100 percent. Situations where fish are stacked in a particular area may make it tempting to go over the limit just a little—or sometimes a lot. It is important to realize many other anglers use these spots too, and just a few anglers keeping too many fish can have an impact on the resources. If we all stay legal, these wintertime hotspots should stay productive for many years to come.

There is more to winter trout fishing than warm water discharges. Anglers wanting to fish the jetties in winter should give the boat cuts a shot. Other good spots include any deep holes on both the channel and Gulf side of the jetty wall.

At the short rigs a few trout can be caught during winter. One of the best methods is to pitch a 1/4-ounce jighead dressed with a piece of shrimp against the pilings. If you're looking for larger trout, consider fishing with chunks of cut bait on the bottom. It may sound weird, but it can catch fish.

SHIP CHANNEL SECRETS

The red/white Super Spook walked along the shoreline with an almost military like rhythm.

"Splish-splash"
"Splish-splash"
"Splish-splash"

My cousin Frank Moore is a real pro at working this particular plug and as I commented on the smoothness of his presentation, he looked over at his graph and smiled.

"We're marking lots of bait and I'm pretty sure it's mullet," he said without causing his plug to break a stride.

Mullet are exactly what we wanted and as we both worked our topwaters over this big school, we hoped a super-sized sow speck would come out to play.

"Splish-splash"
"Splish-splash"
"Gulp"

Frank's Super Spook disappeared as the water below it boiled with a hint of silver.

"Got one," he said as his rod bent with the stress of something heavy and feisty on the other end. That something turned out to be a 28-inch, eight-pound trout and was one of four nice fish we caught in that spot within 30 minutes. Where were we fishing? It was a spot in the Intracoastal Waterway near Lake Calcasieu that most people probably never consider fishing. In fact, on that day, all of the boats we saw passed us up and headed for Big Lake. We however were content with fishing in what on the surface might seem to be an unusual area.

In the late 1990s, the late Capt. Daniel Pyle turned me on to the big trout you can catch in the ship channel during spring and since then this avenue of fishing has held a special appeal. During late winter and early spring, bay systems do not have much in the way of big bait to offer trout. The shrimp are a non-issue and menhaden are tiny which is why the sand eels that dwell oyster reefs are such an important part of their diets. Studies have shown large specks prefer fish such as mullet, which is why trophy trout purists look for any concentration of them to find their quarry.

There are mullet in the bays in the spring, but you might be surprised to see just how many are hanging out in the ship channels this time of year. If you watch your graph while traversing these areas, you might just be astounded. While fishing with Pyle the first time, we found a school of mullet at least one hundred yards long, parallel to a shoreline I had passed a hundred times and never fished.

That is probably because I never looked at it the right way. Too many anglers, me included, look at what is on the surface and do not pay adequate attention to what is below. You will not find a walleye angler, for example, that does not live and die by his fish finder. Learning what is below and searching for baitfish and game fish are crucial to finding specks in the channels.

There are things visible to the naked eye that will give you a hint as to where the fish might be. First off, if you actually see 'nervous water' or mullet near the surface, that is obviously a good place to start. Secondly, any area that is near a cut or has some kind of water flow into a marsh or lake is definitely worth trying. It does not take a genius to figure out that the exchange of water from shallow to deep makes for a prime spot for predators to catch their prey items. Deer hunters often refer to "edges", where a thicket meets an open field as being a prime spot to get deer. These edges are also present in water and although they may appear different, the effect is the same. Thirdly, pay special attention to points. If there is a major point coming off an island or extending from the shoreline into the channel, chances are it will hold mullet and therefore has the potential to harbor trout as well.

My first choice is Rat-L-Trap, particularly the chrome with a black back for clearer water or a straight up chartreuse version when it is murky—very often in the spring. Make pattern casts parallel to the shoreline as these schools of bait typically stretch out along them. The Rat-L-Trap is a good choice because you can cast it in the wind which is usually bad this time of year and get some distance out of it. Covering lots of water is essential.

If the bait is nervous over a drop-off or a shallow flat, fish a topwater plug. There are many good ones out there but my favorite is the Skitter Walk. Last spring my father and I stopped at one such spot and I had a Skitter Walk blown two feet out of the water on the first cast. I never did catch that fish but fortunately for us it was among friends. When using topwaters, start

Capt. Mike Morgan works a secondary point coming off an island in the Intracoastal Canal. A secondary point is one that cannot be seen by the naked eye or perhaps only on a low tide.

fishing parallel to the shore but then move back, so you can fish the plug from the shallows out past the drop-off. That is very often where the trout are located.

This is typically what you will find when you have water flow entering a channel. The trout will feed right along the edge of the deep where they can hammer the baitfish. This is a great spot to fish topwaters or fish with slow-sinking plugs like a Catch 2000 or a Chatter Tube. If you do use a slow sinker make sure you let it work the shallows first and then fall over the edge of the drop off. Do not think that these drop offs have to be impressive. Some of the most productive are simply where you will have three feet of water dropping off to six. For us that might not seem like much but for a fish that is a significant change even in the context of an area nearby deep water like the Intracoastal Canal.

Points are another crucial area to target. An ideal situation would be to find a sharp point of an island for example that is located near a big marsh with flow entering the channel. What you want to pay attention to is not necessarily the point itself but the "secondary point", which will only be visible via your electronics.

The main point might extend out to three feet of water whereas the point below it might be sitting out in 10 feet of water on a shelf. Baitfish will gather around these points and so will specks that use them as transition zones from shallow to deep. This is a prime spot to try trolling for trout.

Trolling is a popular method on Louisiana's Lake Ponchatrain and it is something I have been doing for the last few years. Tie on a deep diving crankbait like a Bomber 9A or Fat Free Shad and slowly troll over these secondary points. It is important when the fish are not actively feeding to cover lots of water and that is exactly what trolling allows you to do.

I caught a massive trout while trolling a chartreuse-colored Fat Free Shad over the secondary point of an island when there were no visible signs of any feeding activity. However, the graph showed plenty of baitfish about 10 feet down and some larger fish suspended just below them.

After my first mention of trolling for trout in *Texas Fish & Game* magazine, reader John Sweet contacted me about his method for trolling with medium-running crankbaits around the Galveston Jetties:

"I was fishing at the north jetty one day with my son, and as I was running slowly along the wall. I let out my line because I noticed the spool was a bit loose and I would get a backlash. I had a Rat-L-Trap on the other end, and after I let out about 30 yards and started to reel it back in, I noticed there was pressure on the other end. It ended up being a 3-pound speckled trout. I was basically trolling this Rat-L-Trap and caught a fish, so I told my son we might be on to something. That day we trolled along the rocks and caught more than a dozen trout—and no one else seemed to be catching fish."

Later on, he experimented with medium-running crankbaits designed for bass and found them equally effective.

"You want something that is going to be able to reach different levels of the water, and at the jetties I find the trout are very often suspended. So something that can troll down to them will catch them, along with plenty of redfish."

When the current is strong enough, he simply drifts and trolls the crankbaits. When trolling at the jetties, it is important to use good electronics. Novice jetty anglers tend to think trout are present at every rock along the jetty wall, but nothing could be farther from the truth. Trout often bond to specific pieces of structure, and if you can see them, you can troll directly to them.

Many times these fish will be tightly stacked together. Last year while fishing the Galveston jetties, the only place we would get a trout to bite was between two large rocks. If we threw anywhere else, the only thing that would take our live shrimp was gafftopsail catfish. Another reason for electronics is it is important to look for subtle structure. When looking at a jetty it is obvious there is a lot of structure around the top. However, there is usually plenty more structure and trout around the base. The rocks typically extend out three times farther at the bottom of a jetty. That means if the jetties are 10 feet wide at the top, they are 30 feet wide at the bottom.

Many times trout will hover around one small piece of rock. At the Sabine jetties, they gather around a small boat wreck that sits about 10 feet away from the jetty.

Bass anglers often talk about fishing the "secondary points" of a reservoir. They are talking about fishing points not visible to the naked eye, but are obvious underwater. I think of these small pieces of structure as "secondary points" and look for them first. If there are no trout there, then I can always back off and fish the "main point," which would be the visible and obvious parts of the jetty. I have used crankbaits for trolling and had some success. I used a Hellbender, which is a deep water plug designed for walleye and striped bass up north. Ironically, the first fish I caught on it was a big striper in the Intracoastal Canal. It has also caught a few nice specks for me during winter, when they are deep along the channel. I simply looked for big balls of baitfish on the graph, trolled right over those spots, and caught some specks.

Using deep-diving crankbaits, anglers can get to trout in the channel when bay systems are flooded. We often hear the complaint, "The trout are out deep since it's flooded." Well, why not go after them? Saltwater is heavier than freshwater, so using deep-diving crankbaits can allow you to get down to the trout in deeper water. This is very similar to what northern anglers do when walleye hang around the thermocline in reservoirs. They simply troll for them when pitching jigs or fishing live bait would be impractical.

Trolling live bait for trout can be effective, too. This is something anglers in Mississippi do frequently. The best way is with a downrigger, which most Texans do not own. The poor man's alternative is what I call a breakaway rig. This requires using two rod and reels. One is to fish with, and the other is to get your bait down to the desired depth. Hook a finger mullet, large mud minnow, or croaker through the lips with a small circle hook on braided line. Rig the other rod with a 1-ounce weight attached to a good swivel. Let out some line on the baited rod, then attach the line to the eye of the swivel on the big weight on the other rod with a thin rubber band. Let out enough line to get the big weight to the desired depth. When a fish strikes, it will cut the thin rubber band on the tough, braided line and let you fight the fish freely. The rubber band will remain attached to the swivel, so you are not littering in the process.

This might take awhile to get used to, but it will allow you to troll live baits and perhaps reach fish you never thought catchable. Troll live baits slowly. You might want to start by using your trolling motor, then if that is not doing the trick, crank up the big motor to speed things up a bit.

While researching trolling methods, I came across one very similar to the pattern Louisiana anglers use to catch specks on Lake Pontchartrain. It comes from a British fishing website called "Fishing in Norfolk" and it is something that anyone can do.

According to the site: "One of the great ways of imparting a bit more action in lures or dead baits when trolling either on engines or oars is by using the S trolling pattern. This simple trolling pattern will really put extra fish in your boat, it's that effective.

"Simply position your rods at various depths and start moving in a straight line. After a few meters, maneuver your boat either left or right for a short period, and then simply turn the other way moving in an S pattern, this will allow your baits and lures to move at different speeds and heights in the water thereby giving a more erratic movement to them."

This is a great method for locating fish if you do not know the depth they are holding. Trolling for trout is something that could really catch on in Texas if anglers gave it a chance. I have found it is possible to catch trout in the deep water during the winter with it, and as mentioned earlier, it might be a way of reaching fish pushed out of the bays and into deep water by spring flooding.

The possibilities are endless, so I hope you giving trout trolling a try. You have nothing to lose—and possibly some super speck fishing to gain.

As we all know, late winter and early spring fishing can be challenging on the bays. The ship channels can offer some protection from the wind and sometimes hold surprising numbers of specks. I'm not going to tell you I would rather fish the channel than a nice shallow shoreline covered with good bottom on the bay. I will say the ship channels however have something different to offer and if we all experiment a bit might find that we have all been missing something quite exciting.

chapter three

Understanding Tides:
Why the moon and sun make a difference

Tides are the most misunderstood element of fishing for speckled trout or any other type of saltwater fishing.

As Outdoors Editor of the *Port Arthur News* and Executive Editor of *Texas Fish & Game* magazine, readers frequently contact me with questions regarding what they have seen on tide charts posted on television and in various publications. There is much misinformation and misunderstanding regarding how and when tides move, and what natural forces influence them. One of the questions I hear most often goes something like this: "I saw where the low tide was going to be at 11:15, but the water was up above the boat dock. How could the tide be so high during the low tide period?"

To answer this and any question about tides, it is best to take a good, long look at what tides are and exactly what forces cause them.

Tides are the periodic rise and fall of all ocean waters. One force causes them: gravity—from the moon, sun, and earth.

Saltwater Strategies Book Series: **TEXAS TROUT TACTICS**

Catching trout by the light—and gravitational pull—of the moon.

My mentor, veteran outdoor writer Ed Holder, told me that the easiest way to understand how these tidal movements work is to compare them to a wave: "In essence, a tide is a large, slow-moving wave that starts off in the ocean, moves through a pass, and ends up in the back of a bay or upland into a river system. And it's all influenced by the elements."

Remember, too, that waves are influenced by wind, and tides are no different. This is why some low tides are not always so low. A strong southerly wind pushes a lot of water into a bay system, causing unusually high tides even when moon or solar patterns call for low tides. The difference can be as much as a foot. Conversely, north winds push water out of the bays. That is why autumn brings such low tides. "Blue northers" in conjunction with a strong tidal pull drain bays and estuaries and help to cleanse coastal marshes.

Moving on, but keeping with the idea of the tide as a wave, it is important for anglers to understand that tidal strength at points away from the immediate coastline won't be as strong as those at a pass near the Gulf. "You've got to realize that, like any wave, a tide weakens as it move inland," Holder told me. "So your strongest tide will be near the Gulf and the weakest will be far into the bay or river."

For the *Port Arthur News* our tide charts are for the Old Coast Guard Station at Sabine Pass. However, at Stewt's Island, on the north end of Sabine Lake, a 3-foot tide change at the pass may be reduced to somewhere between two and 2-1/2 feet. Ten miles upriver at the I-10 bridge at the Neches River, it might be only a one-foot change. Remember that the wave weakens as it moves farther inland.

Another question I am frequently asked is: "We saw on the television where we would have a high tide around 5:00 a.m., so we got out there an hour early and the tide didn't move for hours. Was the TV tide table wrong?"

Probably not. Most times when I get a question like this, it's from someone who doesn't understand one very important point: Tides provided in some papers and on television merely tell you when the lows and highs occur. They do not tell you how much change will occur between tides. For instance, say for a Tuesday, the tables predict two high tides and two low tides. The highs will occur at 3:35 a.m. and

12:58 p.m., and the lows at 8:55 a.m. and 8:37 p.m. That is all the information you get in some tables. However, if you dig deeper into charts provided by the National Weather Service, you find some very interesting information about those same tides, such as the tide is forecast to drop only eight inches between the 3:35 am. high and 8:55 a.m. low. In addition, it is forecast to rise only about five inches between the 8:55 a.m. low and 12:50 p.m. high. You would also learn that between that 12:50 p.m. high and the 8:37 p.m. low, the tide is forecast to drop more than 2-1/2 feet, which is a very strong tide for the Texas Gulf Coast.

Now suppose someone decides to go fishing on that Tuesday morning and does not look at our tide chart, but instead glances at the tide times on television. He sees there will be a low tide at 8:55 a.m. and a

Tidal movement is always most pronounced and visible around passes and inlets.

high tide at 12:50 p.m., so he assumes the tide at the Port O'Connor jetties will be rising between those two times. It will, but only five inches, which is an inch an hour. He probably will not even notice the change, and will come back convinced the television was wrong.

When you base a fishing trip around tidal movements, the key thing to watch is the how much change will occur between tides. Just reading the general tide table is a waste of time. An angler must use the tidal correction table to adjust for tidal movements in the area he plans to fish.

TARGETING TROUT AROUND TIDES

Once reading tide charts is mastered, there are some things to keep in mind that can help you fish for trout around tides. It is important to check the charts for quick tidal turnarounds and swings from one extreme to the other in a short period. The faster the water is moving, the more prey is displaced from cover and put into the open water.

Jetty fishing is often more productive on the Gulf side during an incoming tide, but the action shifts to the channel side on an outgoing. This is because shrimp, shad, and other baitfish are flushed from the bay toward the Gulf. Remember that tidal movement is always most out of proportion and visible around passes and inlets—water in these narrow areas is forced through powerfully. However, in the bays or in the ocean, it is not always easy to tell when the current is moving or in which direction.

Sometimes there is a conflict between wind and tide, and on a weak tide with a strong wind, it can be especially hard to tell which force is moving which way. A good way to discern which way the tide is moving is to find some structure and look for signs of movement around it. If you are wading, kick up some sand and see which direction it settles. If in a boat, pitch out a light, sinking lure and see which

Waves are primarily created by wind but are also the product of underwater geologic forces such as earthquakes and volcanic eruptions.

way it moves.

Something I noticed while fishing a few years ago was that during high tides trout were holding super tight to the shorelines on the Louisiana shoreline of Sabine Lake. At the time they were biting and the next day they have lockjaw, or so I thought. The pattern was there. There were gulls working over schools of trout all over the lake one day and then no gulls (or trout on the main lake) at all the next.

While fishing with Mike Tennian of L&S Lures, I headed to the banks between Whisky Bayou and the Pines and found trout literally stacked against the shore. Most of the time trout are known for working out from the shorelines, but they were so tight to the bank that my partners and I were getting hits literally inches from the mud line.

We were fishing with the Mirrolure Catch 5 and a variety of topwaters and caught the most fish by fishing them with a fast retrieve parallel to the shorelines. Most of the time you will cast toward the shore, but once we figured out the fish were literally hugging the bank, we switched to casting down the shoreline to maximize the fishing action.

The areas that held the most trout were where there was a concentration of shad mixed in with shrimp. We found lots of shad with minimal trout, but when there were some shrimp skipping the top of the water as well, the specks were present. The whole scenario had me scratching my head because my theory has been that trout prefer easy access over hard work and on the main body of the bay I could have swam like a fish and caught shad in my mouth. That is how thick they were.

The next week I returned to do some wadefishing in that area and noticed something interesting about the bottom in this location. Over about 100-yard stretch between two well-defined points, the bottom dropped off steeply into some big potholes. I went from my waist deep to chest deep and then rose up to my knees. What I realized is that when Hurricane Rita blew through the area, it changed the bottom in this spot and made it deeper.

Then I got to looking at the cuts coming from the marsh. At the time, the tide was coming in strongly and was quite high which was the same situation that Tennian and I encountered before. I noticed there were a couple of small eddies in relation to the new ridges and potholes formed in the storm. The trout were feeding there because the shrimp and shad gathered in the eddie and at that point were probably trapped there by the feeding trout.

This made perfect sense. That Louisiana shoreline tends to form eddies on tides on incoming tides around cuts, but they are usually small and filled with flounder. Because this location had several small cuts and major changes in topography, it formed a large eddie that is one giant pot of seafood gumbo for marauding specks.

The next weekend, I got to fish with legendary tournament angler Ted Takasaki of Minnesota and we started our adventure at the north levee at Pleasure Island off Sabine Lake. Once again, the fish we caught were tight to the shoreline but this time up against the rocks of the levee.

While talking with some anglers that fished that same stretch of shoreline I learned the fish had been tight to the rocks and biting best on a falling tide all that week. We caught the fish there on Old Bayside Shrimp fished under popping corks and around concentrations of mullet and ladyfish. The bait was using the rocks for cover on the high tides and the trout were taking advantage when the tides receded.

If trout also use structure and tides in conjunction to corral and attack baitfish, then it would make perfect sense, they would use it as an ambush point.

The most important thing to keep in mind is that tides move baitfish around. Big, incoming tides provide great trout fishing during spring and summer, and outgoing tides provide the best action in the fall when cold fronts blow large amounts of water and baitfish out of marshes and into bay systems. In general, the biggest tides provide for the best fishing, no matter if they are high or low—the bigger the better.

Chapter 3 | Understanding Tides

For jetty fishing, the inside (ship channel) side is typically better for trout on an outgoing tide, and the outside (Gulf) is best when the tide is coming back in.

I have seen this work firsthand on several occasions during long summer days when my fishing buddies and I fished both tides. Once, we caught the tail end of an outgoing tide and did well on trout on the inside of the Sabine jetties, and then the tide stopped for about an hour. Nothing happened. We could not even get a hardhead to hit our bait. Then, when the tide started to come back in, we fished the Gulf side and hammered them. Sometimes, tidal movements are important for a particular area for simpler reasons. Shallow flats, for example, have no water on them when tides are low. For fish to be there, water has to be present.

My favorite reason for studying tides is that I do not have to get up at 4:00 a.m. to go fishing all the time. I have often slept as late as 10:00 a.m., ate breakfast, drove down to the boat launch, started fishing around noon, and caught plenty of fish. This is usually about the time everyone else is coming in for the day. That is, except for those savvy salts who know it is tidal movement, not time of day that dictates when trout will bite.

Somewhat differently than tides, waves are created by two forces: geologic forces, such as earthquakes, underwater landslides, and underwater volcanic eruptions. The second—and most common— wave-making force is wind. There are five different kinds of waves: ripples (small rolling waves), whitecaps (the top of the wave is broken off), chops (medium waves), swells (large powerful waves), fully developed, sea-huge waves (tidal wave or sea surge).

Lunar tides are the principle cause of tides, because the moon is closer to the earth than the sun. Solar tides are only about 46% as strong as lunar tides. Tides can be estimated because of their repetitive pattern. A lunar day is 24 hours, 50 minutes, and 28 seconds. Solar years are 365 days long. Due to this pattern, tides can be estimated and charts made to foretell them.

Tides may seem mysterious, but they are a science, and hence predictable and useable to enhance your catching vs. fishing ratio.

chapter four

Tackle:
Selecting rods, reels and line

Getting geared up to go trout fishing has become quite technical over the years. There are so many products on the market that seem like "must haves," and there are many, many specialty fishing tactics to go along with the gear. I personally would hate to be a beginner coming into the sport now, especially if I had no real knowledge of fishing.

It might seem like a six-figure job and a nuclear physics degree is required to get quality trout fishing tackle, but that is not true at all. Getting good gear is not always an easy choice, but it is not on par with choosing the right person to marry. Actually, I know a few fishermen who view it as that important, but they are another story entirely. Perhaps in another book.

REEL SELECTION

For beginners and advanced anglers, there have been tremendous improvements in both spinning and casting reels with huge strides

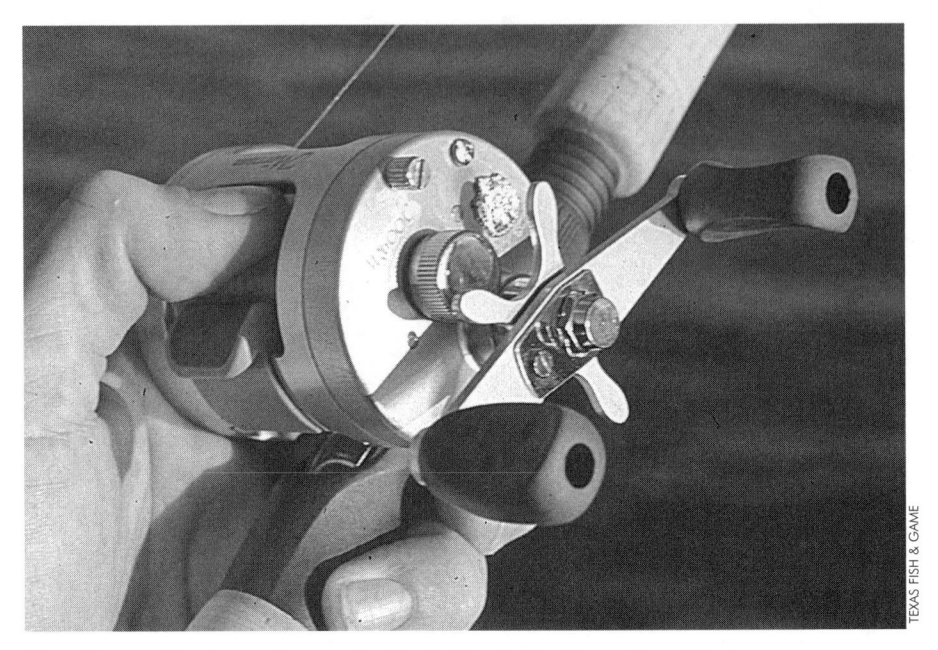

Many Texas saltwater anglers prefer the baitcaster for its casting distance.

made on the drag systems and external components. Most bait-casting reels contain anti-backlash mechanisms that make fishing much easier than when I grew up fishing with my old red Ambassador 5000. Anglers do not have to thumb the spool to prevent it from overrunning or causing a backlash. Backlash-free reels employ magnets that help to work things out for the angler.

Bait-casting reels are by far the most popular in my home state of Texas, but on other parts of the coast, spinning reels are the weapons of choice. Bait-casting reels offer the advantage of casting great distances (although a skilled spinning reel enthusiast like myself can give a diehard bait-caster a run for his money) and overall power.

Spinning reels have also evolved and are much more efficient than they used to be. A spinning reel operates with the line coming off in coils and the spool staying motionless during the cast, unlike a bait-casting reel. Spinning reels have improved with the enhanced tough-

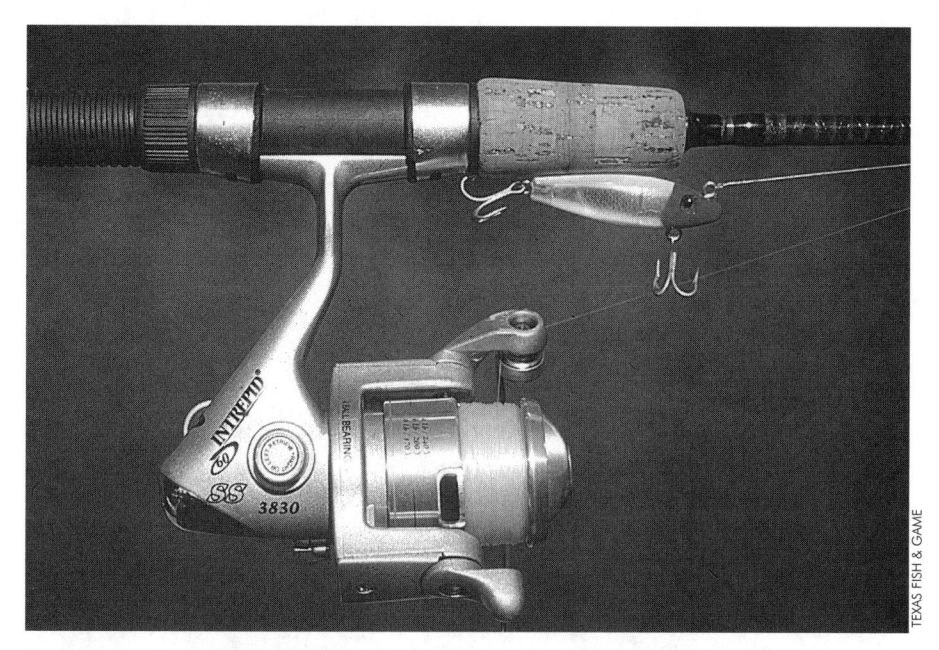

Spinning reels are better for beginners because of less likely backlashes.

ness of roller bearings. They get lots of friction since the line passes over the roller with lots of pressure on a retrieve. The line pickup on older spinning reels scarred the line. Thank God for titanium alloys.

Spinning reels were designed for higher speed retrieves than baitcasters. This has some to do with the gears, but has more to do with line take-up on the rotation of the handle. The wider diameter of a spinning reel spool offers an advantage over rotation at a comparable gear ratio on a casting reel.

Generally speaking, the more line put on a spool the faster the retrieve. Spinning reels are great for beginners because they rarely backlash, (I say "rarely" because sometimes they do, and when this happens, watch out: It's UGLY and, yes, I mean U-G-L-Y) and they are great for finesse fishing with light line and slow-sinkers like the MirrOlure Catch 2000, or flipping Bass Assassins around rocks at the jetties.

The downside of spinning tackle is that after the line sits on the spool for a while, it comes off in tight coils. This is called "line memory." When this happens, you will have to change the line or stretch it by putting a weight on it and dragging it behind the boat for a few minutes.

CHOOSING A ROD

Each rod and reel has its own function. You can't use a heavy action rod to fish with 1/16-ounce tube jigs or use a buggy whip-like light action rod for chunking heavy spoons.

Rod selection, for the most part, should be based on common sense, such as comfort and what type (and weight) of lure will be fished.

The first thing to consider is comfort. If you are 5 feet tall, using a 7-foot rod would be kind of goofy. Likewise, it would be senseless for me at 6-foot-1 to use a 5-foot rod. I can get a whole lot more out of a longer stick. Matching a rod to your body size will improve your lure or bait presentation, give you confidence, and produce less fatigue after a long day on the water.

Rods are partly designed to help you feel the bite of a fish. The blanks or shafts are made from fiberglass, graphite, or some other material or composite. The actions are listed as light, medium, medium/heavy, and heavy. The blank is mounted with eyes, handle, and reel seat to complete the package.

Most of the rod selection process is just common sense. If you are fishing with bait on the bottom in heavy current in deep water, a medium/heavy or heavy action would be appropriate. If finessing slow-biting fish with small lures, give a light action a try. Mediums are good for all kinds of applications from throwing soft plastics to topwater plugs and crankbaits. Most of this falls under the common sense banner and, luckily for novices, many rods now list which kind of lures should be thrown with them.

Again, light action rods are not normally used to fish for trout because strength is needed to pull the fish out of heavy currents. They do have certain applications but are rarely used by most anglers. For topwaters or soft plastic lures, a rod with a fast-action tip and medium/heavy rating would be good. Heavy action rods are best used for fishing bait in deep water.

Do not fall into the trap of thinking you have to buy the most expensive rod out there. Many times the old adage of "you get what you pay for" is true with cheap rods, but there are some fine ones on the market that stand up to any fish. While fishing for peacock bass in South America, I used a $15 no-name rod I bought at an Academy store. The guy I was fishing with had a $400 rod and said he liked the way mine felt and wanted to know how much it cost. When I told him it cost $15, he laughed and said he was going to buy the company.

Line Selection

There are so many brands, sizes, colors, and varieties of fishing lines on the market today, it can be truly mind-boggling. Some of them are good for all-around fishing while others are excellent for very specific applications. I will cover the best kinds for trout fishing.

Super Lines

Most so-called "super lines" are actually braided lines, but there are some fusion lines that are very hard to define, so I will refer to them all as "super lines." In my opinion, certain super lines are the most effective lines for bagging speckled trout or any other kind of game fish. Why? Because they have virtually no stretch, and the most crucial point in an encounter with a fish is hookset.

Another advantage of these lines is you can get a lot of power out of them, which comes in handy if you are fishing the surf and hook into a wayward blacktip shark or tarpon. There are "super lines" out there that are the equivalent diameter of 6-pound-test monofilament but rated 20-pound-test. That is pretty neat stuff if you ask me.

Since about 1996, many of my reels are spooled with some kind of super line, especially the spinning reels. My personal favorite is Berkley Fireline, but Spiderwire, Spider Fusion, Power Pro, and Tough Line are all worth giving a try. Something to keep in mind with these super lines is that many of them come in greenish colors. On my home body of water, Sabine Lake, most of the trout will hardly look at a bait or lure fished on a green line. They're line-shy for some reason. When I use smoke-colored Fireline, I get bites.

Braided, or "super" lines come in handy when fishing in the surf.

In my first book, *Flounder Fundamentals*, I noted that while fishing with my cousin, Frank Moore, in one of the hottest flounder spots in existence, he outfished me 2 to 1 while using smoke-colored Fireline. At the time, I was using a new green color and could hardly get a bite. When we switched rods, the roles reversed, and he could not get a bite. Try to match the line color to the water. The water on Sabine is always brown, so the smoke matches up better.

While no-stretch properties are the biggest advantage of super lines, it is also their biggest drawback. If your drag is set too tight, there

Mark Davis of Big Water Adventures caught this huge trout on a Badonk-A-Donk near Port Mansfield. The clear water in that area often demands anglers use fluorocarbon leaders because the fish tend to get line shy.

is a good chance you will loose the fish at the hookset. There must be some give, or you are defeating the purpose of these super strong lines. While fishing with super lines, I have found them great for topwater applications. I like to have a lot of contact with a topwater plug, and the enhanced sensitivity of these lines certainly provides that. It also takes some of the guesswork out of setting the hook.

Before mastering the art of fishing with super lines, I lost many speckled trout that hit on topwater plugs. I would get so excited when the fish hit that I would jerk the lure out of its mouth. This is a cardinal mistake, but what can I say? I am easily excitable around trout. While fishing with Capt. George Knighten in the Chandeleur Islands, I learned to simply let the fish take the bait and hook itself. My hook-to-land ratio went up tremendously. Now, when using super lines I simply let the fish take it under, count to three, and sternly pull the rod back to set the hook. This is a stark contrast to yanking the rod back as soon as a fish hits. I call this "Bill Dancing." When I was a kid, I got a kick out of the bass fishing superstar making these tremendous, dramatic hooksets. My term is certainly meant as no disrespect to Dance; I think he is great at what he does, but every time I tell someone to stop "Bill Dancing" their fish, they get it. I guess I wasn't the only one that noticed.

I said goofing up the hookset by setting the drag too tight with super lines was the main drawback, but there is another: backlash. If you get a backlash with braided or fusion line, forget it. Get out the knife and start cutting because you are not going to get that thing out. I use braided line on spinning reels most of the time, so I do not have much of a backlash problem, but friends of mine who use it on casting reels are converting to backlash-free models. Capt. Terry Shaunessy of the Hackberry Rod & Gun Club said he puts a backing of monofilament on his reel spools then layers the braid on top. He said this cuts down on backlash problems in a big way.

Some might disagree that fluorocarbon line does not belong in the "super line" category, but I will put it in here anyway. It has some super properties. Fluorocarbon line has been commonly used for years, especially in clear water areas like South Florida and by fly-fishermen who pursue wary trout species in clear northern streams. This stuff is nearly invisible in the water. It gets its name from a chemical called, you guessed it, fluorocarbon. It has close to the same light refraction rate as water, which makes it disappear once below the surface.

Recently, I have used a fluorocarbon-coated line called P-Line to great success—and I use it in the toughest of situations. I have always said fishing line that can stand up to offshore species caught around oil rigs can stand up anywhere. The species caught offshore fight harder and grow larger than their inshore counterparts, and the barnacle-encrusted oil rig pilings make these areas even more challenging.

For a test write-up in *Texas Fish & Game* magazine, I took out some of the P-Line CXX X-TRA Strong fishing line to the oil rigs out of Galveston. I had fished with the original P-line, a super strong monofilament, in Venezuela in December 1999 and found it great for yanking big peacock bass out of the brushy, flooded rainforest around Lake Guri. I wanted to see if the CXX X-TRA Strong would yield the same results in the Gulf, and it did.

P-line is an in-between ground for anglers who don't know which way to go. Its stealth qualities help tremendously

MONOFILAMENT

There is nothing wrong with using monofilament. Many companies have improved their monofilament greatly over the last few years. Stren's Sensor and Berkley's Big Game are some that come to mind as excellent choices. These have very low-stretch properties and little line memory.

When considering a specific brand of monofilament, always keep in mind stretch and abrasion resistance. As mentioned earlier, color is also critical. I would stick with something clear, but the Triple Fish line, which is camouflage, is intriguing. I have used it on a couple of trips to the short rigs out of Sabine Pass and found it excellent. I did not catch any more or less fish using it, so I call that success.

There is no reason to go in-depth about monofilament line, as most of the ones on the market are of great quality and will get the job done. Just keep in mind that most of the time you want to use as light a line as you can get away with for speckled trout fishing. Going ultra-light is crazy unless you want the thrill of playing a fish, but if you want to actually land them, set your drag and use something that can han-

For trout, use the lightest monofilament you can get away with.

dle most any fish. Something like 12- or 14-pound test can handle anything out there as long as you have your drag set properly. In most applications, there is no need to go heavier for trout. That is what "super lines" are for.

AVOIDING LINE PROBLEMS

One can never be too prepared for fishing. One way to maximize our time on the water is to make sure that equipment problems are identified and fixed on land, not standing in the bay.

Many fish are missed because of bad fishing line. I am not talking about bad brands of line, but line in bad condition. A weak line is a fish's greatest ally.

Over time, monofilament on a reel starts coming off in loops instead of in a smooth flow, and it can become brittle. If you can change your line at least once a year, depending on your dedication to fishing, you can avoid this problem.

Fish teeth can play heck with line. Fish often make nicks invisible to the naked eye, but that can result in a lost fish later down the road. After catching a fish, particularly a toothy one, run the last few feet of line through your lips and feel for abrasion. If you feel any roughness, break off and retie.

Nothing is worse for your line or reels than direct sunlight or the heat of a car trunk. Keep them in a cool dark place when you are not on the water.

Line twist is almost unavoidable because it's caused by so many factors. Lures that twist, such as plastic worms with hooks off-center, and spoons and spinners are common culprits. You also can twist line with a spinning reel when you continue to turn the handle while the drag is slipping; every turn of the rotor puts a full twist in the line.

No matter what causes the twist, it's easy to remove, according to the experts at Stren. They suggest you remove all terminal tackle and troll the bare line behind your boat for a few minutes. The current running over the line quickly takes out the twist.

HOOK SELECTION

Writing about hooks gets messy. There are so many different brands, sizes, and models that it is difficult to keep up with them and make timely recommendations. I might recommend a 4/0 hook and three companies have three different size hooks of the same supposed standard. What I will stick with in this selection are some hooks I use and tips from my personal experience.

For live bait fishing, I prefer Kahle-style hooks, which are the ones that are slightly curved on the shank. I find I get a much better hookset and catch more than I do with standard J-style hooks. I also get to live release far more fish. Kahle hooks tend catch in the corner of a

Anglers who want to release big fish to produce more of their kind should consider foregoing treble hooks even on their plugs. Capt. Bruce Shuler of Port Mansfield replaces all of his treble hooks with singles even on topwaters and said he sees very little difference in catch rates.

fish's mouth, and with catch-and-release so popular, this is a valuable feature. Also, with more and more restrictive size limits, using a hook that does not deep-hook is very ethical. I hate to release fish I know are going to die.

With that said, treble hooks are flat-out fish killers. That is not a bad thing if you are catching fish to eat, but if you must release, there are problems. The Texas Parks & Wildlife Department published a paper in 1984 citing studies showing a mortality rate of up to 55.6 percent for trout caught on treble hooks. Another study showed a 37 percent death rate for trout caught on a variety of gear. In other words, if you are fishing with live bait and want to release fish, treble hooks are a bad idea. If you are using topwaters or other lures with treble hooks, you might want to consider bending or filing down the barbs if you are catch-and-release conscious.

For red snapper and other species, I have long been a proponent of circle hooks, which some call "Japanese hooks." This term is used because the hooks were popularized by Japanese commercial fishermen. Although they do not look like they could be used for much of anything productive, circle hooks provide anglers with a higher chance of actually hooking a fish and offer the advantage of not hooking deep. This increases the chance of survival if catch-and-release is the goal. Most circle hooks are used offshore, but there are small ones that I am experimenting with for live bait trout fishing. Until then, I have found a good stand-in.

Daiichi has a hook called the Tru-Turn that acts in much the same way as a circle hook, but it looks a lot more like a standard hook. I have tested this thing on redfish and sharks, which are notorious for swallowing hooks, and out of more than 50 bull reds and nearly 100 sharks caught on the hook, I've had only one fish (a large shark) swallow it.

No matter what kind of hook you use, make sure it is sharp. A dull hook is as sure a way to loose a fish as any, which is why I always carry a sharpener along with me on fishing adventures.

chapter five

Lures:
The allure of metal and plastic fakery

Trout are more receptive to artificial lures than any other coast-dwelling species. The snook may be a close second in terms of lure friendliness, but the trout is the bona fide king of plastic. Trout are every bit as receptive to lures as largemouth bass and have spawned hundreds of live bait imitations.

This chapter is devoted to reviewing some of the lures I've found most effective for trout. Some of them I've used for years, some were suggested by experts, and others I tried specifically for this book. There are simply too many lures and subtle variations to cover the strengths and weaknesses of each type within a genre. However, the synopses below apply to other lures of similar configuration.

GULP! SHRIMP

COLOR: New penny, white
BEST SEASON(S): Year-round
APPLICATION/LOCATION: Anywhere, any time
TECHNIQUE: Gulp! can be fished under a popping cork over seagrass beds or on the main body of a bay, on a jighead or a Fish Finder Rig.
TIPS: Gulp! works amazingly well and creates a scent envelope of sorts that makes it work like live bait. In an early field test with its inventors I out fished them using Gulp! while they had live shrimp. Avoid fishing in areas with heavy concentrations of hardheads and croaker because they will nail it as well.

The Gulp! Shrimp is arguably the most effective lure available to anglers now. In nearly two decades of outdoors coverage, the author has never seen anything like the Gulp! phenomenon in terms of popularity.

CORKY DEVIL

BEST SEASON(S): Winter, early Spring
COLOR: Various colors are effective.
APPLICATION/LOCATION: This lure is a slow-sinker, so it's best in no-to-moderate current. Flats and eddies in the mouths of marshy cuts are good places to fish this lure.
TECHNIQUE: Throw it, let it sink, twitch gently, and let it hit bottom. Trout hit this lure on the fall.
TIPS: Fish it slow, slow, slow.

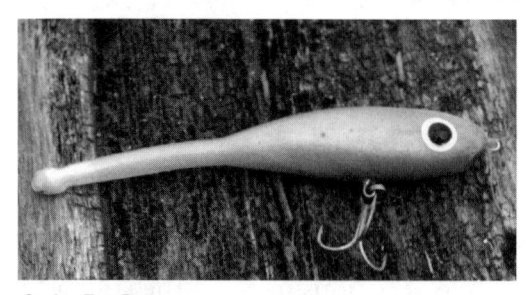

Corky Fat Boy

CRÈME KILLER DILLER

COLOR: clear, glow/chartreuse
BEST SEASON(S): Year-round
APPLICATION/LOCATION: Anywhere, anytime.
TECHNIQUE: Fish on a free-line rig or under a popping cork. This is the one of the best shrimp imitations I have ever fished.

Chapter 5 | Lures

TIPS: During winter, crawl the lure slowly across the bottom to draw strikes from huge trout.

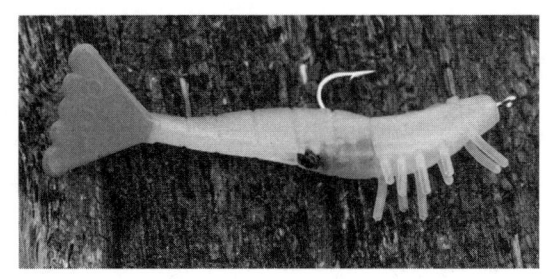

Créme Killer Diller

RAPALA SKITTER WALK

COLOR: Various colors are effective.
BEST SEASON(S): Year-round
APPLICATION/LOCATION: Use anywhere trout are liable to hit topwaters.
TECHNIQUE: Walk the dog slow or fast.

Rapala Skitter Walk

TIPS: This is an easy plug to walk so you can get more distance out of it than most. If you make long casts, use a braided line so you get no stretch and more hookups.

MIRROLURE TOP DOG

COLOR: bone, black, chartreuse
BEST SEASON(S): Year-round
APPLICATION/LOCATION: Anywhere topwater action is expected.
TECHNIQUE: Walk the dog, plain and simple.
TIPS: The Top Dog is one of the most popular lures of all time, and for good reason. It's easy to walk, cast, and catch fish on. I like to use it with braided line—the lure walks better and my hook-to-land ratio is increased.

Mirrolure Top Dog

CHUG BUG

COLOR: Various colors are effective.
BEST SEASON(S): Fall
APPLICATION/LOCATION: This lure is excellent for catching schooling trout. It is an underrated lure in my book.

Chug Bug

TECHNIQUE: As the name implies, this lure is a "chugger" at its best with a twitching retrieve to make the cupped face splash and "chug." The combination of motion and sound are the hallmarks of this type of lure.
TIPS: Don't try to walk it, chug it.

RAT-L-TRAP

COLOR: chrome/blue, chrome/black
BEST SEASON(S): Year-round
APPLICATION/LOCATION: Tie one on and rip through the water. This lure can also be fished under a popping cork and drifted over shell. This is popular in Southwest Louisiana, especially on Lake Calcasieu.

Rat-L-Trap

TECHNIQUE: This is a good fish-finding lure that can cover a lot of water quickly. It's hard to go wrong fishing this lure.
TIPS: In the Winter, I have caught good trout by letting this lure hit the bottom and then retrieving slowly.

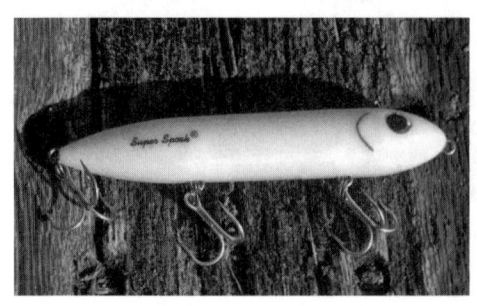

SUPER SPOOK

COLOR: bone with red head
BEST SEASON(S): Year-round
APPLICATION/LOCATION: Anywhere topwater action is expected.
TECHNIQUE: Walk the dog or twitch and pause. I find this lure displaces water differently than a Top Dog and some other lures.

Super Spook

Chapter 5 | Lures

By twitching and pausing, you can entice some of those lazy and skittish trout into hitting.

TIPS: Paint large eyes on both sides of the head. It works. It may look weird, but it seems to have an affect on the fish.

MIRROLURE CATCH 2000

COLOR: Various colors are effective.

BEST SEASON(S): Winter, early Spring

APPLICATION/LOCATION: This lure is awesome for catching big sow trout. It's a slow, slow sinker and easier to fish than some slow sinkers.

Mirrolure Catch 2000

TECHNIQUE: Throw it, let it sink, sink, sink, pop it, let it sink some more, then retrieve.

TIPS: If you think you're fishing slowly, slow down some more.

TEXAS TROUT KILLER

COLOR: Various colors are effective.

BEST SEASON(S): Spring, Summer, Fall

APPLICATION/LOCATION: This is a good lure for fishing oyster reefs in the Spring and under gulls in the Fall.

Texas Trout Killer

TECHNIQUE: Put it on a jighead and work like any other soft plastic lure.

TIPS: Use as light a jighead as possible.

BASS ASSASSIN

COLOR: I like darker colors such as red shad and morning glory.

BEST SEASON(S): Winter, early Spring

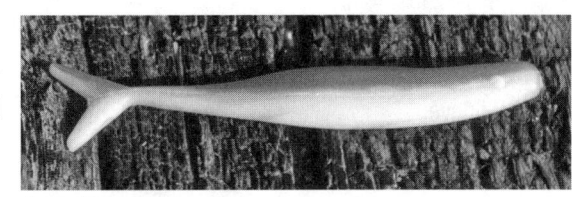

Bass Assassin

APPLICATION/LOCATION: This is a fairly slow-sinking soft plastic that can be fished without a jighead. Use it in areas where trout are slow to respond to topwaters or other soft plastics.
TECHNIQUE: Fish with a very slow retrieve.
TIPS: Try this lure rigged "wacky style." This means hooking the lure in the center and letting it sink without a weight. It works great for bass, and I have caught trout this way.

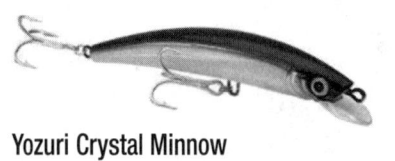

YOZURI CRYSTAL MINNOW

Yozuri Crystal Minnow

COLOR: red/white, black/silver, rainbow trout
BEST SEASON(S): Spring, Summer
APPLICATION/LOCATION: This is a highly detailed lure that works great for taking trout that won't hit topwaters or plastics.
TECHNIQUE: It can be fished lots of different ways. I like to just reel it in slowly.
TIPS: Don't lose this lure—it's expensive.

YOZURI MAG POPPER

COLOR: Various colors are effective.
BEST SEASON(S): Summer, Fall
APPLICATION/LOCATION: Use anywhere trout are surface feeding.
TECHNIQUE: Pop slowly or skid the lure across the water.
TIPS: Tie on with a loop knot to enhance the action.

STORM WILDEYE

Storm Wildeye

COLOR: croaker pattern
BEST SEASON(S): Spring, Winter
APPLICATION/LOCATION: Fish anywhere trout might be hungry.
TECHNIQUE: This is a good one to rig on a jighead and skip slowly across the bottom of a mud flat.
TIPS: Fish slow.

MIRROLURE 51 AND 52

COLOR: Various colors are effective.
BEST SEASON(S): Winter, Spring, Summer
APPLICATION/LOCATION: This lure can be fished effectively virtually anywhere.
TECHNIQUE: The 51MR, 52M, and 52MR sink at a rate of one foot per second. It's best to use the 51MR series because the line attachment is in the nose, which gives better control. Great wade-fishing lure.
TIPS: The 68M Deep Runner is a heavier 52M style. Use it when fishing deeper water or areas with a lot of current. The sink rate is approximately two feet per second.

FOOLER

COLOR: glow, chartreuse
BEST SEASON(S): Spring, Summer, Fall
APPLICATION/LOCATION: Best fished under birds and around schooling fish.
TECHNIQUE: Put it on a jighead and pop it as you would any other soft plastic. It's also great fished under a popping cork.
TIPS: If the trout are striking short, cut off the first half-inch to shorten the lure.

SLIMY SLUG

COLOR: fire tiger, tomato
BEST SEASON(S): Spring
APPLICATION/LOCATION: Slimy Slugs are excellent for fishing over oyster reefs when bay systems are muddy. They imitate sand eels well.
TECHNIQUE: Rig it on jighead and drift-fish.
TIPS: Can also be fished "wacky style" under birds.

Slimy Slug

RIP TIDE WEEDLESS SHRIMP

BEST SEASON(S): summer, early fall
COLOR: smoke red mist, pearl glow, chartreuse
APPLICATION/LOCATION: Since it's weedless, this is a good lure to fish in the marsh during high tides. The marshes are filled with shrimp, and this is a weedless imitator.
TECHNIQUE: Throw around clumps of grass in marshes and other areas with heavy vegetation. Aim for specific areas and work thoroughly.
TIPS: Don't be afraid to drag through heavy grass. The lure is designed for this kind of fishing.

DOA Bait Buster

DOA BAIT BUSTER

COLOR: white with red, chartreuse
BEST SEASON(S): Year-round
APPLICATION/LOCATION: This is a fairly slow sinker good for fishing in the surf and in shallow areas.
TECHNIQUE: Drag it slowly across the bottom.
TIPS: DOA Lures inventor Mark Nichols says to fish this lure "slower than evolution." He means it.

Twister Tail

TWISTER TAIL

COLOR: white, chartreuse, glow, pearl
BEST SEASON(S): Spring, Summer, Fall
APPLICATION/LOCATION: This lure is best fished on a 1/8- or 1/4-ounce jighead around the mouths of marsh points and along bay shorelines. This is not a good lure in heavy current.
TECHNIQUE: Drag slowly or hop it across the bottom.
TIPS: There is another version of this lure called the Spin Top combo that has a slightly different jighead and a small teardrop-bladed spinner fitted on it. It's hard to find, but an excellent lure.

NORTON SAND EEL
BEST SEASON(S): Spring
COLOR: glow/chartreuse, pearl
APPLICATION/LOCATION: This lure is a fine imitator of the sand eel, which is a chief prey item for trout in early Spring. It can catch trout anywhere, but is best fished over oyster reefs.
TECHNIQUE: I've found this lure most effective when fished on a 3/8-ounce jighead and bounced on the bottom.
TIPS: When fishing oyster reefs with this lure, try to keep your retrieve as slow as possible. Reefs are often located in areas with heavy current and a too-fast retrieve causes missed strikes. Don't expect to catch lots of trout on an oyster reef; it's size that counts here.

BILL LEWIS SLAPSTICK
BEST SEASON(S): Spring, Summer, Fall
COLOR: chrome, chrome back, chartreuse shiner
APPLICATION/LOCATION: This lure is best fished in shallow water where trout are visibly feeding. Flats and shallow points are ideal.
TECHNIQUE: This tail-heavy lure sits upright in the water. Throw it in the vicinity of feeding trout, pop once, and pause. Lather, rinse, and repeat.
TIPS: Allow trout to take lure under before setting hook. When you do set the hook, do it hard.

DOA TERROR-EYZ
BEST SEASON(S): Spring, Summer
COLOR: chartreuse, white, red and white
APPLICATION/LOCATION: This is a good lure to pitch into stand of cane along shorelines and to work eddies.
TECHNIQUE: For best results, I usually slowly hop it across the bottom.
TIPS: The lure is designed for special jigheads with red, protruding eyes. Therefore, I like to fish it in the clearest water possible to get the full effect.

DOA Terror-Eyz

PYGMY SPIN

BEST SEASON(S): Spring

COLOR: silver scale, fluorescent red/white

APPLICATION/LOCATION: This is a good lure in areas with large concentrations of small menhaden.

TECHNIQUE: Fish with a slow retrieve, casting parallel to productive shorelines and into eddies.

Pygmy Spin

Tips: Don't be surprised to catch redfish on this lure. It's a killer in the marsh.

SHAD ASSASSIN

BEST SEASON(S): Summer, Fall

COLOR: chartreuse, pearl

APPLICATION/LOCATION: This one is best on the main body of a bay in front of marshy drains thick with large menhaden, mullet, and shrimp.

Shad Assasin

TECHNIQUE: Like other soft plastics, this one is best fished on a jighead and bounced across the bottom.

TIPS: Match the hatch. If you're fishing around lots of shad (menhaden), go to this lure. It works.

CULPRIT DT WORM

BEST SEASON(S): Spring, Summer, Fall

COLOR: pearl, tequila shad, pumpkinseed

APPLICATION/LOCATION: This is a double-tailed worm designed for bass fishing, but it makes a great crossover into saltwater. I like to fish it in heavy current to give the lure more action.

TECHNIQUE: This is a go-to lure when the trout simply won't bite but I know they're in an area. I use what is called a "dead

Culprit DT Worm

Chapter 5 | Lures

worm" technique in bass fishing. It consists of throwing the lure out and letting it sit, then slowly retrieving and letting it sit again. In current, the tail of this lure gives up incredible action.
TIPS: Use a heavy jighead for heavy current. Go with at least a 3/8-ounce, upgrading to 1/2-ounce if needed.

JOHNSON 1/2-OUNCE SPOON
BEST SEASON(S): Summer, Fall
COLOR: silver
APPLICATION/LOCATION: This one is best fished on a flat where trout are actively feeding. Don't use this lure to find trout.
TECHNIQUE: Use a variable retrieve. Throw to areas where trout are visibly attacking baitfish.
TIPS: It wouldn't hurt to dress this lure with a red skirt or chartreuse Twister Tail trailer.

BERKLEY POWER MULLET
BEST SEASON(S): Summer, Fall
COLOR: glow/chartreuse, purple/yellow (for murky conditions)
APPLICATION/LOCATION: A good lure for fishing in river systems above bays, where trout sometimes gather when salinity levels are high.
TECHNIQUE: This lure works best on a fish-finder (Carolina) rig, but makes a good bottom-bouncer, too.
TIPS: Don't be afraid to let trout take this lure. It's flavored like a real fish, so fish hold it longer.

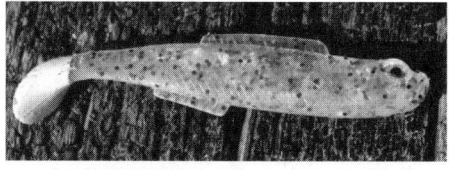

Berkley Power Mullet

BANJO MINNOW
BEST SEASON(S): Summer, Fall
COLOR: natural minnow
APPLICATION/LOCATION: This is a large lure that's good in heavy current. I wouldn't hesitate to fish it at jetties or in large drainages.
TECHNIQUE: Slowly drag across the bottom on a jig head or with special Banjo Minnow weight across the bottom.
TIPS: Possibly the liveliest lure I've seen. Don't overwork—it moves enough on its own.

CT MULLET

BEST SEASON(S): Spring, Summer, Fall
COLOR: pumpkin/chartreuse, glow/white
APPLICATION/LOCATION: This is a good lure for oyster reefs and drainage flows.
TECHNIQUE: Like most plastics, drag or bounce across the bottom.
TIPS: I like to rig this one perpendicular to the hook.

SEBILE SPLASHER

COLOR: Various colors.
BEST Season(s): Year-round
APPLICATION/LOCATION: This is the best mass produced chugger I have ever fished.
TECHNIQUE: This plug really creates a splash and is a good fish finder on those days nothing else seems to work. In my experience it draws surface strikes when other lures will not. It is not something I fish on every trip but always have one ready to tie on.
TIPS: Do not overwork it. Fish slow for the best reaction.

Sebile Splasher

SASSY SHAD

Best SEASON(S): Spring, Summer, Fall
COLOR: natural shad, pearl, chartreuse
APPLICATION/LOCATION: In Spring, use the smallest version in eddies where small baitfishes go to rest. During Summer and Fall, go to the big 5-inch version to target trout feeding on large menhaden.
TECHNIQUE: Drag it slowly or hop it on the bottom.
TIPS: Be mindful of size for the different seasons. You've got to "match the hatch," so to speak. Small in Spring and larger in Summer and Fall is the rule.

Sassy Shad

SPIT-N-IMAGE

BEST SEASON(S): Spring, Summer, Fall
COLOR: Tennessee shad, red/white
APPLICATION/LOCATION: This is an effective lure only when trout area actively feeding.
TECHNIQUE: Throw it, pop a few times, and reel in a few feet.
TIPS: I don't like to pop this lure too much. I sometimes skip it across the water.

Spit-N-Image

CHUGGING ALONG

"We're not bass fishing Chester."

That was the reaction I got last winter when some friends of mine and I decided to go catch some winter trout on West Galveston Bay.

"Chuggers are for old guys."

"Get with the times."

I heard it all that morning but soon their words were silenced by the beautiful "sploosh" of a speck sucking under my chugger, a custom plug called the Pop-N-Run.

I didn't out fish all of my friends using walkers that day but I did manage to get a higher blow-up to land ratio.

Back when I first started fishing heavily with topwaters, I was given some Rattlin' Chug Bugs to test and had great success. Since that time, I started fishing walking plugs like the Skitter Walk and She Dog much more but recently I have found myself getting back to chuggers, particularly during winter.

Chuggers are highly underrated for catching big trout and during the winter, their more leisurely pace loud "sploosh" can grab the attention of big sows in the bays. That is why I got a better blowup to hookup ratio on the day described above. We often think of fish as voracious predators that cannot wait to get their mouths on whatever bait or lure we offer them. Reality is much different. We must remember that fish are cold-blooded and water temperatures dictate how they feed and respond to lures.

During winter on the Gulf Coast, water temperatures can run anywhere from the upper 40s to the upper 60s. In a short time span, that is great fluctuation and it can become a challenge for anglers to catch speckled trout. With that in mind, I believe anglers should stick to fishing lures as slow as they can. Even when the water temperature is up, it will allow them to score as trout and other predators are programmed genetically to take the easiest prey items, and one that is moving slowly is the most likely to get hit. Many angler rush to tie on their walking plugs to experience the glorious "blowup" of a big speck. They are certainly effective, but I believe anglers should fish them slower than they normally do. I have been experimenting with fishing with chuggers and have had good success by fishing as slowly as possible.

During winter, I start by using the following pattern: Cast. Chug. Wait five seconds. Chug again.

Then if that doesn't work, use the same pattern but wait only three seconds. It is difficult to fish this way, since it is a lot more fun to make a topwater move fast, but crawling it along can be super effective. Start fishing your plugs with a slow retrieve and increase gradually. Never fish as fast as you would in summer or fall. Even on warm days, trout are not as active as they are during those warmer periods. Despite this relative inactivity, some of the best trout of the year are caught.

"A chugger makes you fish a little slower," said noted wildlife photographer and avid angler Gerald Burleigh.

"I have been using them for years for largemouth bass and always caught really nice fish often when others were missing them or getting short strikes. Then I started using them for trout and doing better than I did on walkers, at least for the larger fish."

Burleigh compares big sow specks to Florida largemouth bass and believes if anglers studied this strain of largemouths a bit they would get a better perspective on big trout.

"I have ponds stocked with Florida bass on my property and the first thing you learn is the more Florida's you have, the less fish you are going to catch. Sure, they will get bigger but part of their genetics is they simply do not bite as much, which is probably why they get bigger: less are taken from the population."

"When you translate that to big trout, you are getting to the top of the gene pool. The big ones that made it to trophy size got there for a reason and I believe part of it is they are programmed not to bite as much as their counterparts do. A chugger more naturally mimics what a wounded baitfish would be doing in cold months which is why I like fishing them," Burleigh said.

I agree wholeheartedly with this principle and find the parallels to largemouth bass fishing dead on, especially in regards to genetics. The Texas Parks & Wildlife Department for years has been tinkering with genetics to create a strain of largemouths that would more readily bite angler's lures and baits for stocking in urban community lakes. They know Florida's get lockjaw soon in life and I believe there is a dividing line on trout from a genetic perspective to simply be more cautious. I don't think most fish "learn" with age. Studies have shown their memories are very short, however, genetic programming could be the answer to why certain fish get big and others don't. I do not think it is all growth genes although that is certainly part of it, but also a caution gene that makes them less likely to end up hooked.

With that said, looking into this issue has strengthened my theory that chuggers are overlooked and could perhaps lead to far more trophy trout caught by anglers, particularly those less skilled at using walking plugs. Let's face it, not everyone can properly "walk the dog" but anyone can fish a chugger.

I like to use them on super lines like Berkley Fireline or Spider Wire because my style of hookset involves no true hookset. We miss many trout because as soon as we see the blowup we rear back, trying to set the hook with only water in way of the hooks. In reality, most blowups are misses and we get the fish on the second or maybe third strike, so give the fish some time. I had to learn this lesson back in the 1990s while fishing in the Chandeleur Islands and getting only 1/3 of the fish that blew up on the Top Dog I was fishing. The guys I was fishing with were very patient anglers and simply let the fish hook themselves and started reeling in when they did.

With a super line with no stretch, you can do this easily. I let the fish strike and when it starts to run with the plug, I steadily raise my rod tip and start reeling in, rarely miss fish when I do so. When there is no stretch in the line, there is no give and therefore hooks go where they need to go.

If you start seeing signs of trout feeding or hear the familiar "gulp!" of a big sow sucking under a mullet, tie on a chugger and get ready.

The Upside of Topwaters

A shark cage in the Pacific Ocean might seem like a strange place to think about topwater plugs, but while watching the crew of our vessel pull a yellow and red surfboard above me, I could not help but relate it to topwater fishing.

Since chumming is illegal where we were diving with great white sharks, surfboards are used to mimic seals in much the same way anglers pull chugging topwaters to imitate wounded baitfishes. As I waited for the real life "Jaws" to show up, I thought, I hope sharks like yellow, because I can't see the red on top.

Then it hit me: If I could not see the red, could a speckled trout or largemouth bass see the back of a topwater plug?

Many times, anglers insist back colors are crucial in lure selection--but are they really. When would the fish ever see it, and even if part of the back dips into the water, would it make a difference?

This inspired me to venture below the surface to photograph topwaters from a fish's perspective and to answer my own question: Does back color make a difference?

Here are my observations:

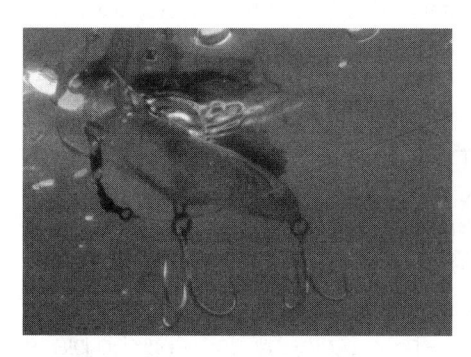

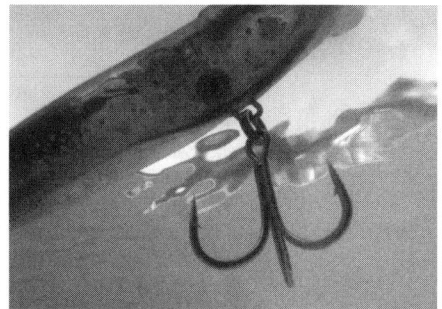

LURE: Sebile Splasher
TYPE: chugger
VISIBILITY: 2-1/2 feet in sandy green water
PERSPECTIVE: just in front of and below lure
OBSERVATIONS: The clear body and black back create a very realistic look combined with Sebile's fluid and glitter-like innards. The black back creates an easy point of contrast, and even in less than optimal water conditions, the lure puts off a strong reflection.

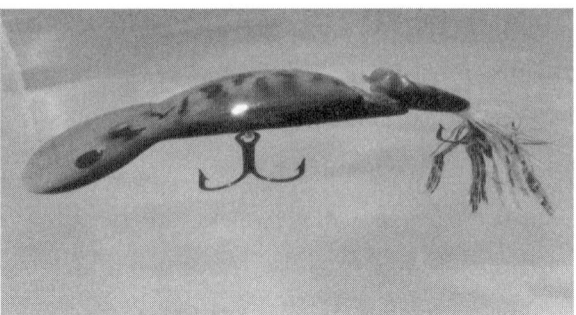

LURE: Injured Minda
TYPE: surface/sub surface
VISIBILITY: 10 feet
PERSPECTIVE: 2 feet away, dead on
OBSERVATIONS: This is the lure in its diving position and on the surface. It can be fished in one spot and rise back slowly to the surface. In clear water, the lure had a powerful contrast and the green/black outlines made it visible from as far away as 10 feet.

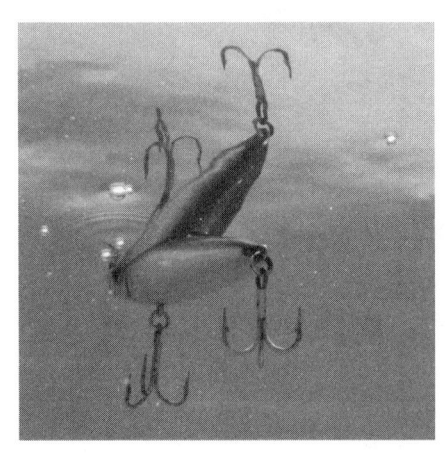

LURE: MirrOlure Top Dog
TYPE: walker
VISIBILITY: 3 feet in green water
PERSPECTIVE: 2-1/2 feet away, 2 feet down from behind
OBSERVATIONS: This photo was taken on a cloudy day, and the black back and orange belly made a striking contrast. It also put off a very visible reflection.

Chapter 5 | Lures

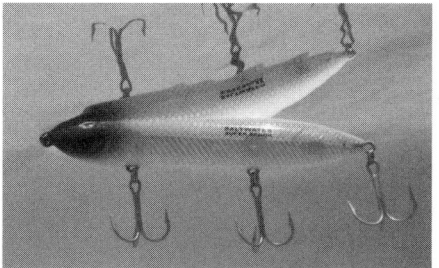

LURE: Super Spook
TYPE: walker
VISIBILITY: 10 feet
PERSPECTIVE: 3 feet away directly below lure, and 2 feet below/2 feet away
OBSERVATIONS: This lure does not have a contrasting back color, but I thought it would be interesting to see an underwater perspective of the red/white contrast on the head since it is such a popular combination in Texas. From a distance of 10 feet, the (human) eye is drawn directly to the red/white line on the head. It also put off an impressive reflection.

CONCLUSIONS

I believe sound is the main attractor of predatory fish to topwaters. However, even in semi-murky water, certain visual cues likely trigger bites from elusive big fish that make few mistakes. Young fish will strike at anything, but big ones require more convincing.

The back color of a topwater can make a big difference in visibility. Most plugs sit with their heads out of the water and tail end sloping down just below the surface, and when done in conjunction with contrasting colors, gives fish something on which to focus. The surface of the surfboard mentioned at the beginning of the story was red, but it stayed totally on the surface and the sharks could not have seen it. With these topwaters, the back was visible.

Another artifact of sloping backs and contrast line was a well-defined reflection. How often have you been fishing a topwater and had a fish strike but miss the plug, even in clear water? Is it possible they could be striking at the reflection?

After this experiment, I have concluded back color and other lines of contrast can be an important factor in topwater fishing success. I would not have thought so a few years ago, but that was before I put on my dive mask and looked at things from the perspective of a fish. While we cannot mimic fish eyesight, approaching a topwater as they do reveals things we simply cannot see from our normal perspective.

At this point, you might be wondering if I ever saw a great white shark hit that surfboard. Yes, I did--four times, in fact, and it was life changing.

Comparing a great white's "blow-up" to even the most powerful topwater strikers such as peacock bass is like comparing a hand grenade to an atom bomb. While watching the great sharks slam the surfboard with relentless aggression, I was totally immersed in the moment, but walked away with motivation to study the topwaters we use here in Texas.

How cool is that?

THE SECRET BEHIND GULP!

Back in 2005, I was presented with some Berkley Gulp! shrimp to test while spending some time at Shoal Grass Lodge in Aransas Pass. I had passed the product on the shelves in various stores and heard a lot of buzz about it, hailing it as a "new level of artificial lures."

The package claimed Gulp! outperformed live bait, which to me was highly questionable. I am extremely cautious of such claims and felt there was no way this was possible. At about the time those thoughts crossed my mind, Capt. Bobby Caskey, owner of Shoal Grass Lodge, stepped into my room to tell me we would wake up at 5:30 a.m. for

Chapter 5 | Lures

breakfast and then enjoy a day of fishing.

"I see you've got some Gulp! there," Caskey said. "There are some guys fishing the Gulp! crabs for bull redfish out in the surf and they claim it is working miracles for them."

At that point I decided I could not wait until morning to see how this stuff worked, so I grabbed my rod and reel, carried a package of Gulp! down to the dock and commenced a field test. My thoughts were that if this stuff worked better than live bait and could catch bull reds in the surf; there was one way to find out how good it was: cut it up in chunks and see if the pinfish and sheepshead would hit it. I could throw practically any soft plastic around the dock all night and catch speckled trout, but by simply soaking a little chunk of soft plastic material around the dock, I would probably catch nothing. A live shrimp would likely succumb to the pinfish quickly, so I figured this would be a good test.

I cut up a Gulp! shrimp into five pieces, placed one on a hook, and lowered it into the water. Within seconds, my rod twitched and a big pinfish was pulling on the other end. This process repeated until I had caught over half a dozen pinfish and one nice sheepshead on the Gulp! That is, I caught those fish on little chunks of Gulp! just like what might happen if dead or live shrimp were on the hook. At this point, I was intrigued and figured there might be something to the hype.

Later, I returned to Shoal Grass to fish with some of the people from Pure Fishing, Blackjack Boats, Bill Kenner, and Danny Goyen of Goyen's Guide Service. Karen Anfinson and I fished together, and we had the idea to put live bait against Gulp! She would fish with live shrimp and I would fish strictly with Gulp!

The wind blew relentlessly all day, making casting and bite detection difficult, but every time we found a protected piece of shoreline, we found redfish and speckled trout. Moreover, at the end of the day, I out-fished Karen by a nice margin fishing with Gulp!

Later that night, I got to pick the brain of Gulp! inventor, John Prochnow, who has worked for Berkley/Pure Fishing for a number of years. His insight into this phenomenon shed light on what makes an artificial produce like the real thing.

"We started working on this about 17 years ago," Prochnow said. We put a team together to produce something like this, and came up with two versions of what we thought might work. However, issues like shelf life came up and we could not meet all of the expectations of the anglers.

"We needed a substitute for PVC, and there were a number of other companies that had biodegradable baits, stuff like Chewy Juice and Crappie Candy. However, those were very hard, stiff and unreasonable for the angler. Very early on, we learned that anglers would not compromise if you couldn't deliver all of the properties they need."

Prochnow said they decided as a company their product had to perform better, which eventually resulted in Gulp!: "The analogy is, if you are eating lunch and you eat a sack lunch, you take it out of the bag and eat it. That's what Gulp! is like. If you leave it in the sandwich bag, It's like a lot of the other stuff out there.

"Gulp! is a water permeable matrix; a sponge, if you will. We formulate the scent in it, and dissolving out all of the scent and flavor. It has 400 times faster scent and flavor dispersion than anything else. We have proven that. We put a known amount of die in a plastic and in Gulp!, in known volumes of water. That's how you can prove it. Let me tell you, the tests were extremely exhaustive."

A big part of the Gulp! bait's success is creating an effective "scent window."

"In my mind, it looks like about 12 inches around the bait, and the longer you leave it in the water, the greater the scent trail it creates," Prochnow said. "Depending on how active the fish are and how hungry they are, they will follow the trail and eventually bite."

The Pure Fishing team did head-to-head comparisons, having teams of anglers go out together, and fish Gulp! next to live bait with identical tackle.

"Every 20 minutes, we switch tackle. After so many hundred fish you have caught, you can cycle through. We have seen spikes of bait not producing and Gulp! out-producing it," Prochnow said.

In the lab, they used striper, redfish, and pinfish: "We have a patented system that Dr. Jones came up with, where he puts different flavors on cotton pellets, and they are used to get the fish coming in that way. They take it, and if they spit it out, it is no good. We note how long they will hold it, and dilute it to determine which compound is still standing at lower concentrations. We just keep diluting it until one of them doesn't eat it anymore.

"Then we take the baits, cut them into little pieces, and compare it to natural squid. The Gulp! actually outperformed natural fish. We will put down natural bait with six or eight anglers in the back, with a number of baits, and rotating them. By the end of a number of trips, you can determine what is going on, and Gulp! outperformed cigar minnows. It is not just because of the scent and flavor. Gulp! stays on the hook better, but it gets to the bottom past a lot of the trash fish, so not only do you have the scent and flavor technology, but a better delivery system that can get down to the fish."

When asked if in the course of their research if they discovered that there are lots of differences between what fish eat, he used the analogy that different fish will eat different stuff but, "We all eat meat and potatoes. We all have different tastes. The different fish are that same way, but what you season it with is what makes it better for something else. Put meat and potatoes in all of them, so to speak, by utilizing things that appeals to fish across the board. We season it with those flavorants.

"We don't claim that it's just for bass and walleye, for example. We found that saltwater species have their own set of seasonings that they like. We are in the process of upgrading, finding different seasonings so we can widen the appeal to fish, and to anglers pursuing fish in different kinds of situations."

As you can see, a lot of research, work, and thought go into producing a product like Gulp! before it ever hits the market. At that point, the advertising people do their jobs and come up with slogans like "Out-fishes live bait."

At that point, it's up to the angler to decide whether the product lives up to the hype, or is at least worth keeping in their tackle box. After fishing with Gulp! I am not ready to abandon live bait altogether, but I will say it has definitely earned a permanent spot in my tackle box.

LURE ACCESSORIES

Spray-on fish attractants like Fish Formula and some of the others are very effective at keeping a trout's attention. I know guys who spray WD-40 on their lures to juice them up, and they catch fish. I'm not sure how environmentally sound that is, though.

Tube jigs weren't mentioned in the lure reviews because, well, a tube jig is a tube jig. They're great to use throughout the year for trout; remember to go up in size with the seasons. A neat trick is to stuff the tube jig with pieces of Alka-Seltzer and bits of shrimp. It will give off bubbles and scent to help attract fish.

In *Flounder Fundamentals*, I wrote about tipping soft plastic lures with pieces of shrimp. This also works for speckled trout. As with flounder, this gives the trout a reason to hold onto a plastic lure, and leaves a scent trail to lead an out-of-sight fish to the lure. Be sure to use fresh in good condition. If they look like they've been left in the sun for a long time, don't waste your time. Remember, too, that 90 percent of the scent in a shrimp's body is located in the tail section. Use scissors to cut a piece of the tail into small pieces.

MODIFYING LURES

Sometimes it pays to alter fishing lures. I learned this firsthand while fishing with a lure modifying expert Ben Jarrett of Kilgore, Texas a few years ago. "If you want to catch these big fish, you've got to fish with a big-fish specific bait like a Spook or something else with some size," said Jarrett. You'll catch the small ones on these baits too. Then sometimes, like today, they want something a little offbeat. That's why I'm fishing with this modified bait. The regular Spook wasn't getting the job done, and neither was anything else."

Calling Jarrett's bait "offbeat" would be putting it lightly. His Super Spook was painted with large eyes all over the body. It looked like a survivor of the Chernobyl nuclear plant incident, but it seemed to really turn on the fish that day. He said of the weird-looking Spook: "I fully believe in those eyes all over the bait. The sight of the eyes can really trigger a fish to strike. It gets their predator instincts going in a big way. Modifying baits can sometimes make the difference between catching fish, catching lots of fish, or catching really big ones."

This is something that coastal anglers have become increasingly aware of over the past few years. Many anglers no longer rely entirely on lure manufacturers to produce specific colors, shapes, and actions. They modify lures according to conditions in the waters they fish.

Jarrett's multi-eyed Super Spook is just one of many topwater variations I have heard of or seen. While visiting a tackle store in Venice, Louisiana, I met a man who super-glued pieces of red ribbon just behind the eyes of his Top Dog. He said this was to imitate bleeding gills. He said he only used the bait in summer because low oxygen conditions caused gill problems with mullet in the area. He said the trout and redfish fed on these weak mullet, and that's why he came up with the modification.

A very interesting topwater modification was sent to me by a reader of my "Outdoors Page" in the *Port Arthur News*. He links three Rattlin' Chug Bugs together with 80-pound-test Spiderwire. The first lure is a Big Bug, the second is the standard, and the third a Baby Bug. He said it imitates a school of baitfish. He simply pops or chugs the lure instead of walking the dog. Judging from the digital picture he sent me of some of the fish he caught on the contraption, I may try it myself.

Soft plastic lures are easy to modify and are often subjects of experimentation. The simplest modification is trimming length or appendages to "match the hatch" so a bait more closely approximates the size or configuration of whatever the trout are eating. Another easy modification is on-the-water color changes, which can be made with the Colorite Bait Coloring System produced by the Colorite Bait Company of Alvin, Texas. I found that one of my favorite colors for topwaters is anything with a red head and white body. Once I got the Colorite system, I translated this over to plastics by dipping the first half-inch of a white shrimp tail in red tail dip. The stuff dries almost instantly and stays on well, which makes it practical to carry along on a fishing trip for last-minute modifications.

One of the neatest modifications I have seen was used by a bass fisherman from Kentucky. When fishing a Texas rig for bass, he rigs up with two worms instead of one. He puts on a barrel swivel and then connects two hooks and bullet weights on 1-foot leaders. He claims this drives the bass crazy and helped him to win several small fishing tournaments.

I considered using this for saltwater fishing with Norton Sand Eels or Culprit Worms, which are both excellent lures for imitating the eels common to Texas oyster reefs. I pour some of my own jigheads, so I made some heads with double hooks, which, by the way, are very difficult to find. I'll simply fish the lures on a common head and see what happens. For anglers who don't have their own equipment for this, just use the Texas-rig method above. It will produce about the same action as a double-hook jighead, and it might be fun to tell your buddies you smoked the trout on a Texas-rigged worm. They may not believe you, but that doesn't matter if you catch fish.

Mark Nichols, of DOA Lures, and I talked about modifying his Adjusta-Floater by fishing it on a Carolina rig. For salty anglers unfamiliar with bass fishing lingo, a Carolina rig is freshwater lingo for a fish-finder rig. It consists of an egg weight above a swivel and finished off with a leader and hook. An Adjusta-Floater should suspend well with this modification and drive those finicky fish crazy. This rig also works for suspending stick- or crankbaits. In fact, Mark Davis of Shakespeare did this very thing while fishing a Fat Free Shad crankbait at Lake Aqua Milpa in Mexico, and caught several bass.

The simple addition of a popping cork can give a lure an entirely different life—or save its life, so to speak. While drift-fishing over heavy grass or structure, it pays to fish a Rat-L-Trap under a popping cork, especially during winter when fish metabolisms are slow. The movement of the current should keep the action going, and by using a cork, it helps you stay away from tangles.

The same thing could be done with a Corky. Since they're virtually impossible to find, working a Corky under a cork might be a good way of keeping the lure from getting lost, and add some new action to the bait. Before writing this chapter, I rigged up a Corky under a cork and chunked into my buddy's swimming pool. I rigged the lure four feet under the cork and watched it go. The Corky still got plenty of action, so I don't know why this method wouldn't work.

Call me crazy, call me strange, but these modifications can and do work. Sometimes fish don't' like to cooperate, so we have to encourage them a little. I say, when it comes to lure fishing, the motto should be: "By any means necessary." That includes the weird stuff.

chapter six

Live bait:
When all else fails—and even when it doesn't

Live bait is the most effective means of catching speckled trout. This is not true in every scenario, but if a person were starving and had to catch specks to survive, live bait would be the way to go. It is hard to outdo nature, even with modern technology. Some purists mistakenly believe there is not much to fishing with bait. "Any dummy can hook a shrimp" and "Croaker soaking takes no talent" are a couple of the comments I have heard over the years. In my experience and observations, this is nonsense.

There are numerous ways to utilize live bait and there are many, many good live baits out there. Live bait is not a magic bullet, but sometimes, it is pretty close.

SHRIMP

Most people don't believe in magic, but after witnessing anglers yanking one big trout after another from the Texas side of the Sabine jetties, East Galveston Bay, Lake Calcasieu, and Laguna Madre over the years, I do.

Live shrimp is magical for speckled trout in many situations. Those that have had access to this precious commodity tend to bring home truly impressive catches when others are struggling. A prime example is a trip to the Sabine jetties where my cousin, Frank Moore, and I caught lots of big redfish, but struggled to catch trout while some gentlemen down the rocks caught one after another; many of them were huge. The difference was live shrimp.

We arranged for our friend, David Kinser, to bring live shrimp from Galveston Bay two days later, but we were not able to match their magic. The water was milk chocolate when Kinser came down and we struggled to catch trout, although the ones we did catch were big ones. Yes, live shrimp can catch lots of trout, but, like any mystical potion, it takes other ingredients to make the brew. One crucial ingredient in the Sabine jetty cauldron is clear water.

The words "clear water" doesn't mean it has to look like tap water. It is rare to get water that clear in the Sabine area, but being able to see your bait a few feet down is a good indication conditions are right. At the beginning of this chapter, I mentioned that live bait isn't necessarily a cinch, and this is exactly the point. An angler must learn what water conditions work with particular live bait in the chosen destination. This may take a few failed trips to learn, but such is the nature of fishing.

My favorite ways to rig shrimp are under a weighted popping cork and on a free line rig with a 1/8-ounce split shot weight 6 inches above a Kahle hook. I prefer the free line rig, but using a cork has its advantages in many situations, including helping avoid hang-ups on jetty rocks and oyster reefs.

Castnets are invaluable asset for anglers using live bait. It is far less expensive to catch your own than buy at a bait shop.

CROAKER

Croaker may be the single best bait for catching large speckled trout. Shrimp is responsible for catching more trout than any other live bait, but croaker catches more big fish than other live bait. My first experience with croaker was nearly a decade ago while fishing with Mike Daleo of Sour Lake, Texas. He was and is an avid trout fisherman, and kept telling me we would hammer the trout on croaker. We fished croaker and live shrimp and, to put it mildly, we hammered 'em. Ironically, we caught more fish on shrimp, including the largest fish of the day, a 28-incher. Nonetheless, the croaker proved their worth. We didn't catch a single tiny trout on them, nor any sheepshead or hardheads. The shrimp drew strikes from all kinds of fish.

To be honest, I haven't done much croaker fishing since then, but have no ill will toward those who do. In fact, I jump at the chance to fish with croaker when the opportunity is presented. I like catching fish, and croaker can definitely aid in that department. That's the biggest advantage of croaker. It allows anglers to catch fish, which gets often overlooked in an age when a blowup on a topwater plug (glorious thing that it is) is considered the climax of trout fishing. Anglers not adept at throwing big trout-specific lures can have an excellent shot at catching the fish of a lifetime by simply soaking croaker on the bottom in the Galveston Ship Channel, Baffin Bay, or any other location trout visit.

Piggy Perch

Capt. David Dillman taught me about the advantages of using piggy perch for trout. Shrimp and croaker are better all-around baits, but for fishing at jetties and nearshore oil platforms, these little fish are hard to beat. They can be purchased at some bait camps, but most dedicated piggy users catch their own in traps. Something worth noting about piggies is that some old timers like to clip their sharp dorsal fins before using them for bait. They say it makes it easier for a trout to swallow.

Mud Minnow (Gulf Killifish, Cocahoe Minnow)

Mud minnows are without a doubt the most popular and probably the all-around best flounder bait. These small marsh-dwellers are abundant in flounder territory year-round and are a regular part of their natural diet. Mud minnows are also excellent for trout.

Several years ago, while flounder fishing, I decided to use some leftover mud minnows for trout—and it worked. In fact, the results were tremendous. While drifting a large oyster reef, my father and I used live mud minnows under popping corks. We caught trout weighing from 2 to 5 pounds and limited on redfish. That reef is about 12 feet deep, so we fished our mud minnows halfway down the water column at six feet. On that first mud minnow fishing trip, my father lost one of the biggest trout that ever graced these eyes.

Mud minnows are a very hardy fish that can be hooked several ways: through both lips, behind the dorsal (top) fin, or through the body near the tail. Possibly the biggest advantage to using mud minnows is that they are available year-round at most bait shops when shrimp and croaker can be hard to come by. Mud minnows are also readily caught in traps.

Mullet

Mullet make up a large proportion of large speckled trout's diet, but relatively few anglers use them for bait. I have seen anglers fishing with 8-inch mullet catch mammoth trout over in Southwest Louisiana, where it is very popular bait. The big debate among trout fishermen is what size mullet to use: finger mullet (little ones) or big ones (6- to 8-inchers)? It comes down to what size fish you want to catch. Obviously, large baits deter small fish and entice big ones. If dead set on catching a huge trout, use a huge mullet. If numbers are your game, finger mullet fit the bill. You usually have to catch your own with a cast net. Mullet can be hooked the same way as mud minnows.

Menhaden

Menhaden. Pogey. Shad.

Those are all names used to describe brevoortia patronus arguably the most important link in the food chain in the Gulf of Mexico and highly underrated bait for speckled trout and redfish. Where I am from on the Upper Coast, we call them "shad" and during summer months, they are the "go to" bait choice for many anglers.

I've used shad off and on for many years but first started to consider it a top bait for big specks and reds during the late 1990s when a local tournament essentially became a showcase for anglers fishing with shad. When covering the event for the Port Arthur News and Orange Leader newspapers, the winning anglers would almost always tell me they were using shad either live or "cold".'

The live part is easy to figure out. Hooked through the body, a live shad moves around a lot, emits oil and has a reflective shine that makes it irresistible for predators. The cold choice is a bit different. Unless you have an oxygen diffusion unit for your live well like the Oxygen Edge, it is difficult to keep shad alive during summer months. At some point anglers figured out that by laying shad on top of ice and keeping them dry the fish retain a hookable texture and work just as good as the live version. Most anglers keep the drain plugs in their ice chest pulled so the water goes out instead of engulfing the shad, which makes them mushy once dead.

There are a number of ways to fish these shad, the most popular being under a popping cork. I like to drift the open waters of Sabine Lake during the heat of summer with a cold (or live) shad drifted two feet under an Old Bayside Paradise Popper. This cork is easy to use and its titanium shaft makes it virtually indestructible which is important for anglers like me who tend to be a bit destructive with their own equipment.

"I use those corks a lot and have found them to be indispensable for the summer shad fishery. What we do is drift the open areas in the mid-lake area around large concentrations of shad, which the trout and reds feed on heavily. By presenting them with a wounded shad which is evident by its swimming action or lack of and the oils they emit, with the combination of a loud popping cork above it to get attention, you have the formula for catching lots of fish," said Sabine Lake guide Capt. Skip James.

Some anglers prefer fishing the shad on a Carolina (fish finder) rig, which consists of an egg weight, rigged above a swivel and attached a leader. This method works well in transition zones from cuts to main body of bays and shallow flats coming off islands along the Intracoastal. Rig up an 18-24 inch leader finished off with a sharp kahle-style hook for best results. This fishing can be very productive for trout and reds as well, but it is very tidally driven.

PINFISH

Pinfish are not as good as piggy perch, but they do catch their share of specks. Pinfish are usually caught on hook and line or in traps like piggy perch and mud minnows.

MARINE WORMS

Occasionally, a bait camp will carry marine worms. These creatures are eaten frequently by trout during spring, when these horrible looking creatures are most abundant. They are worth a try if you can find them.

FIDDLER CRABS

Believe it or not, trout eat crab, especially in winter and the very first part of spring when other forage is not available. Fiddler crabs are worthwhile if nothing else is available.

EEL

Eel are tough to come by, but if you are fortunate enough to catch some small ones in a cast net, use them. Trout gorge themselves on small sand eels during the spring period. Think how many soft plastic baits are designed to look like an eel. Trust me, that is not by accident.

Cut Bait

Believe it or not, cut bait is good for catching trout. It is certainly not the bait of choice in most situations, but it is responsible for catching mammoth fish. In 1998, I saw a 9-pounder caught on cut mullet near the mouth of the Neches River. I have caught several nice trout on cut bait while fishing for redfish and alligator gar.

Big trout are slow-moving opportunists, and it seems that a big wad of fresh cut bait waving around in the water is too much for some to resist. A small but dedicated contingent of anglers use cut bait almost

Anglers without recirculating livewells can get away with using ice chests and pure oxygen. The author has used this method many times.

Croaker are the most effective and controversial bait for trophy-sized trout. Some anglers feel they are too effective and have helped decrease the number of huge trout in areas like Baffin Bay.

exclusively in Lower Laguna Madre (mainly cut ballyhoo), and they catch monstrous fish.

BAITING THE HOOK

Placement of the hook in both shrimp and baitfish is very important if you want them to stay alive. Hook shrimp behind the base of the horn or through the collar. On baitfishes, place the hook through the upper lip ahead of its eyes. With larger baitfish, like some mullet and croaker, it is better to hook the fish through the back below the dorsal fin. Some anglers like to hook croaker in the body just ahead of the anal fin.

KEEPING BAIT ALIVE

The trick to using live bait is keeping it alive. A dead baitfish is not nearly as enticing as something that wiggles. For land-bound anglers, a large Styrofoam ice chest does good job keeping most baitfish kicking. Styrofoam breathes and, if the water is changed periodically, most bait will do well. For anglers in boats, a circulating livewell is the ideal setup. By exchanging water frequently, anglers can achieve fairly low bait mortality in most situations. Something that can help is the products produced by Sure-Life Laboratories. They have chemicals called Pogy-Saver, Croaker-Saver, and Shrimp-Saver, as well as stuff designed

Mullet are an excellent bait for trout although their use is mostly restricted to Southeast Texas and Southwest Louisiana.

specially for mullet and many other baitfishes. A couple of spoonfuls of this stuff helps eliminate ammonia in the water, which kills many baitfish.

My father used barely dampened sawdust to keep shrimp alive, and back in the 1970s and early 1980s, some camps sold live shrimp in sawdust. Some, particularly in Florida, still carry on this tradition. Sawdust holds in moisture and actually keeps the shrimp alive longer than just sitting in a regular bait bucket. The strange thing is, it is very important not to dampen the sawdust too much or it kills the shrimp.

THE OXYGEN EDGE

In more than 30 years of research, TPWD has found that low levels of dissolved oxygen kills more fish than any other single cause. Biologists suspect low oxygen causes 60 percent of all fish and other aquatic wildlife mortality. Hypoxia (oxygen depravation) moralities seem to be far more prevalent in saltwater. Some 56 percent of habitat affected by low oxygen is in the Gulf of Mexico, 30 percent is in estuaries, and 14 percent is in freshwater lakes and streams. The potential for fish morality increases dramatically during the summer months when rising water temperatures contribute to lower oxygen levels in coastal waters.

David Kinser, of Anahuac, Texas, has a unique insight into this phenomenon that all anglers can benefit from. An avid angler, Kinser has spent more than two decades creating and modifying human life support systems for the medical field and has developed an uncanny understanding of the links between oxygen, life, and death: "Oxygen is quite simply the key to all life. Without it, nothing can live. That is why all of these space probes and satellites we are sending out into the galaxy are looking for signs of oxygen on other planets. Without oxygen, life as we know it cannot exist."

Saltwater Strategies Book Series: **TEXAS TROUT TACTICS**

Battle lines have been drawn between the "croaker soakers" and "purists" over the use of this deadly-effective bait.

Kinser owns Oxygenation Systems of Texas, and has garnered quite a reputation among live bait enthusiasts and bass tournament anglers for his "Oxygen Edge" fish and bait oxygenation system. Instead of relying on standard aeration to keep bait or tournament fish alive, Kinser's system super-charges the water with pure oxygen:

"Standard aeration systems draw from the air, which is composed of 21 percent oxygen. Factor in that many units only achieve 65 to 80 percent efficiency, and it becomes obvious what happens when water temperatures start to heat up. The fish die because they are not getting enough oxygen."

Having owned an Oxygen Edge unit since early 1998 and I can attest to its absolute effectiveness. Speaking very conservatively, it has reduced live bait mortality in my live well by 80 percent. Another advantage is that it keeps baitfish "super-charged." The oxygen keeps their metabolism so high that they are very frisky and more likely to attract a response from a trout.

BAITING THE ISSUE: THE CROAKER CONTROVERSY

Let's get this over with.

Live bait is controversial among certain groups on the Gulf Coast. Using live croaker is especially disputed among a vocal minority. No word ignites as much heated debate or more greatly polarizes views on conservation and fishing ethics along the coast particular in Texas as "croaker." This pretty, smallish, saltwater panfish has garnered a reputation few if any other fishes have achieved; that of an enabler.

According to the naysayers, it enables ordinary anglers to decimate the speckled trout population in the entire Gulf of Mexico and its bays.

Croaker are not maligned for being great bait stealers or for not growing to epic proportions. They are hated because they are so effective for catching trophy-sized speckled trout. You may ask: "Isn't catching big fish the point of fishing?" In essence it is, but now there are concerns that croaker are a deadly enough bait to put serious strain on trout of superior genetics and thus decrease the overall trophy potential throughout all Texas bays. On one side of the fence, you have the anglers who use croakers. They're called "croaker soakers" by the purists. On the other side, the purists who curse the day Texas anglers discovered the croaker's effectiveness.

As noted earlier in this chapter, croakers are tremendous for catching trophy-sized speckled trout.

The argument is that croaker fishermen specifically target the largest and most prolific breeders from the speckled trout population. Croaker are said to be able to catch big fish when no lure or other bait can. There is also concern that very few croaker fishermen practice catch-and-release. On that note, TPWD has been monitoring the need to limit the number of trout caught by any means, and a big part of this, according to some sources, is due to the popularity of fishing with croaker. Back when the controversy first reared its head Hal Osburn was head of TPWD's coastal fisheries. Here is what he had to say about the croaker controversy.

"Right now things are fine as far as recruitment of new trout into the population, but we're always looking into the status and asking questions about the future of the species," said former TPWD coastal fisheries director Hal Osburn. "If we make a change regarding any fish limits, we're going to limit the number of fish that can be taken or perhaps even a certain size fish like with the slot limit placed on red drum and black drum. We're not quite ready to be in the business of prohibiting certain kinds of bait."

A strong contingent of coastal fishermen wish this was not so, and state their feelings with great conviction. A prime example is an anonymous email I received from a listener to my radio show. He was offended that I mentioned croaker were responsible for some huge trout catches at the Galveston jetties. Here it is in full, unedited glory:

"Chester, you should be ashamed of yourself. By mentioning live croaker on the air, you are promoting the rape of the speckled trout resources. The blood is on your hands. Every year when the croaker soakers start up we start catching fewer big trout. That's because they're catching and killing them with the croaker. It takes no talent to fish with croaker and it's unethical. Shame on all who use croaker and especially on the guides who participate in the rape of the resource on a daily basis [sic]."

I've corresponded with numerous anglers who share similar feelings about the croaker issue. There seems to be a strong mixture of concern over trout populations, and animosity against those who use live bait in general. There is another twist to the story: the endangerment of croaker populations. Thus far, the anti-croaker crowd have gotten nowhere with the Texas Parks & Wildlife Department (TPWD) on the subject of banning croaker as baitfish. Just as TF&G Editor Don Zaidle predicted in August 2006, they will most likely turn to the legislature to sneak in a croaker bait ban under the guise of "croaker conservation."

They tried this once a few years ago, when State Senator Jon Lindsay, R-Houston, introduced Senate Bill 1790. Thankfully, it died in committee, but if enacted, this ridiculous piece of legislation would have banned the use of Atlantic croaker, American stardrum, spot croaker, and sand trout as bait unless the fish is 10 inches or longer.

At the time, the 'Houston Chronicle' quoted Lindsay saying: "My goal with this bill is twofold. One is to take some of the tremendous pressure off speckled trout; use of croaker has decimated the trout in some southern bays. The other goal of the proposed croaker ban is to allow the panfish population to rebound."

This time expect whoever introduces such a bill to dress it up as a bill strictly for "croaker conservation." Remember those two words because you will be hearing a lot about them until the next legislative meets. As anyone with functional brain matter can figure out, the real agenda is to eliminate croaker as a baitfish for speckled trout. Some say it is because croaker use has put too much pressure on speckled trout populations because it is too effective. Right now, however, I want to address the "croaker conservation" movement because it is all a big lie that insults the intelligence of those who are actually concerned with croaker populations.

Since croaker have been a popular baitfish, TPWD has been getting questions about the effect of croaker on trout populations. They have a little Q&A section on their website dedicated to the subject and they address the role of the croaker bait industry on croaker populations. Remember, the "croaker conservationists" are out there saying using croaker for bait is decimating croaker populations.

"The main sector of mortality of croaker is the bycatch in shrimp trawls. We estimate around 390 million croaker are caught and killed annually by the shrimp industry. We estimate up to two to three million croaker are used as bait annually," said Texas Parks & Wildlife Department's (TPWD) science Director, Larry McEachron in the Q&A.

Let's break that down for the anti-croaker crowd.

I will go with the higher end of the estimate and say there are three million croaker used for bait annually. Considering that 390 million are caught in shrimp trawls that would put the alleged impact of the croaker bait industry at less than one percent.

However, this statement is from 2000, so let us say for argument's sake croaker use has tripled in Texas since then (which it has not, not even close) then it is still only at less than one percent of the bycatch. Banning croaker use or, as some of the elitists are trying to do, putting a size limit on croaker would be like putting a band-aid on an amputated arm. You might stop a trickle of blood, but you would still lose gallons.

TPWD agrees and points out that croaker used as bait is simply using a resource that would die anyway in most cases.

On their website for everyone to see, McEachron said, "If it were illegal to use croaker, then these fish would be returned to the water dead. It makes good biological and economic sense to utilize fish as live bait that would otherwise die. The live bait-fish sector of the shrimp industry has little effect on the overall croaker population."

You see if these "croaker conservationists" were really concerned about croaker, they would be lobbying to create stricter bycatch reduction devices and donating to the Saltwater Conservation Association to help them buy back shrimping licenses.

That would help croaker, but banning them as baitfish would only hurt bait shrimpers who in many cases pay their bills with croaker money and more importantly give the government an opportunity to take us down the road of bait banning of all kinds.

Anyone who believes that if we banned croaker as bait it would end there is naïve, very naïve.

For the record, I have only used croaker for trout fishing maybe 10 times in my life. I use artificial lures for trout fishing at least 80 percent of the time and I am truly addicted to topwater fishing.

In other words I really do not have a personal stake in this issue other than the fact I want people to have freedom of bait choice in fishing. If the anti-croaker crowd wants to ban them, they should be intellectually honest and state their reasons outright.

It is laughable to think that people who are outraged about using croaker as bait are suddenly concerned about bringing back the croaker runs of the past and saving a fish they seem to hate so much. By the way, at the time of this writing bycatch in Texas bays and in the Gulf had been reduced significantly due to a buyback program initiated by TPWD (with help from the Coastal Conservation Association), high fuel prices and back to back monster hurricanes wiping out part of the fleet. That has allowed croaker to come back in a big way and the experts are predicting the "croaker runs" that used to be so popular among land bound anglers will return. So much for banning croaker as bait to save the species.

I am vehemently against the prohibition of live bait—*any* live bait. I don't like any bureaucracy telling me how I can fish, and don't like the fact that a ban on croaker could eventually lead to a ban on live shrimp and so on. On the other hand, there is a legitimate reason to worry about croaker fishing affecting the overall average size of trout caught in our bays. It is a perplexing problem.

I am with TPWD officials in believing that a change in trout bag and size limits—if and when it is necessary—is the best route to take on this issue. This is exactly what they did in the Lower Laguna Madre when they cut the trout limit from 10 to 5 and it is the blueprint they should use coast wide.

The croaker haters should like this step, since they routinely criticize the "croaker soakers" for keeping limits of big fish. People who tout their belief in catch-and-release should be all for more restrictive bag and size limits—if their convictions are genuine.

chapter seven

Fly-fishing:
The romantic side of speckled trout fishing

I am no fly-fishing expert and have no delusions about ever being one.

I have caught my share of fish of numerous species on fly gear, and must admit it is quite exhilarating. There is something uniquely romantic about fly-fishing, and when considering catching speckled trout this way, romance turns to downright excitement—serious excitement.

I caught my first trout on a fly rod not too long before this manuscript was completed; it was a milestone in my fishing career. I have fly-fished everywhere from the Little Red River in Arkansas to the Guadalupe River in Central Texas, but none of those experiences compared to the charge I got out of catching a nice trout on a Clouser Minnow in the Sabine National Wildlife Refuge.

Fly-fishing is often viewed as an elitist pursuit because, quite frankly, for years it sort of was. Poor boys fished with cane poles and sat

Saltwater Strategies Book Series: **TEXAS TROUT TACTICS**

Fly-fishing and speckled trout are a tantalizing combination.

on a bucket. Rich guys went fly-fishing. Things are no longer this way, and more and more fishermen on the coast are pursuing speckled trout with a fly rod. The interesting part is, those who fish the flies are really into it. You seldom find a coastal fly-fisherman that is "sort of" interested in the sport. To fly-fishers, it's all or nothing.

With that said, it is worth noting that an angler could starve to death if all he had to eat was trout caught on a fly rod. This is not a numbers game, but a pursuit of finesse, grace, and poise.

This book is not about fly-fishing, and I am not qualified to write a book on the subject. However, I do have a knowledge of the subject and have talked with several veteran fly-fishermen whereby to come up with a list of equipment and tips to get you started in the pursuit of speckled trout—or should I say, "a more romantic pursuit of speckled trout."

FLY-FISHING GEAR

A 6- to 8-weight rod with weight-forward, double-tapered fly line is probably the best bet for trout fishing. I have talked with several fishermen who said any line would work, but several recommended weight-forward line because of good experiences with it.

Some novices might do best to fish with a 9-foot, 9-weight rod, which might be overgunning for smaller trout, but it offers easier castability and greater range. On the Gulf Coast, that comes in handy with the strong winds that prevail much of the year. If a person cannot make good casts, he cannot catch fish. It is that simple.

Purchasing fly-fishing gear is another scenario where you get what you pay for. If you plan on trying this sport, you might want to get an inexpensive saltwater combo, but if you are really into it, more expensive gear is required. All fly-fishing tackle is not created equal; if you are an experienced fly-fisher, I do not need to tell you this—you probably could teach me a few things about the sport.

Nowadays, anglers have a huge selection of flies to choose from, many of which are as effective as they are colorful. While fly-fishing for rainbow trout in the Little Red River in Arkansas, I traded fly notes with a guide who makes his living fly-fishing. Some of the flies we use for speckled trout are very similar to the ones used for rainbows and browns. I thought that was neat because, when I was a little kid, I used to think rainbow and speckled trout were cousins.

Here are some of the best flies for speckled trout. Most of these do double duty on redfish too.

Clouser Minnow - Most saltwater fly-fishermen say if they had only one fly to use, this would be it. It is great in the shallows and in deeper water. I caught my first trout on a chartreuse/white variation.

Deceiver Menhaden - This is another popular fly and one I have fished with. I fished with this one on a 5/0 hook and with a white and pink pattern.

Bay Anchovy - There are many good patterns of small translucent baitfish to choose from. These are great because they come in many sizes and can help you "match the hatch," which is discussed elsewhere in this book. You can get them 1/2-inch long up to 3 inches.

Poppers - Poppers are fun because they are the topwater plugs of the fly-fishing world. Enough said.

Deer Hair Mullet - This is a good one for fishing in marshy areas.

Lefty's Deceiver - This fly is named after fly-fishing legend Lefty

Kreh. It produces when others will not. It is very popular, particularly in Florida.

STEALTH, FLIES, AND THE KAYAK CONNECTION

"Stealth" is becoming a major buzzword in coastal fishing circles. This is especially true among fly-fishing enthusiasts. The fly rod is to fishing what the bow is to hunting in terms of the need to closely approach game. Like the bowhunter who uses camouflage to enhance

In fly-fishing, as in bow hunting, stealth is the name of the game.

his stealth, the fly-fisher has available a form of camouflage in the kayak.

It has long been accepted that trophy speckled trout and shallow-water red drum are sensitive to noises created by clumsy humans. Redfish specialists routinely carpet their boats to minimize noise, and many trophy trout aficionados prefer wading to lessen the chances of spooking a big, yellow-mouthed beauty. Scientists on the East Coast have recently found that sound is a key component in the life cycles of speckled trout and other members of the weakfish family. They have an excellent overall hearing capacity and use a variety of sounds to locate each other during spawning time. Most importantly for anglers, it has been proven that sudden, loud noises (dropped tackle boxes, footsteps, etc.) startle them in shallow water settings.

A growing number of coastal anglers are using kayaks to maneuver in bay, lagoon, and surf systems. These light-weight crafts may look like something out of an Alaskan wilderness film, but they are highly effective right here on the Gulf Coast where the sand meets the surf.

Port O'Connor fishing guide Capt. Everett Johnson believes kayaks may very well be the wave of the future for coastal fishing. "Wade-fishing has been the thing for so long because of the stealth issue," he told me. "People want to be quiet approaching big fish, so they understandably go to the technique they know is effective. There are certain distinct advantages to using a kayak. Besides stealth, there are issues such as physical conditioning and access, which kayaks address."

Let's take stealth first.

Kayaks are sleek, quiet craft that allow anglers to get literally right on top of fish without spooking them. "Someone seated in a kayak can get closer to a big trout or redfish than by any other method I've tried," Johnson said. "I've been within 10 feet of reds and had to sit motion-

Chapter 7 | Fly-fishing

Sleek and quiet, a kayak gives the angler a stealthy edge.

less until they moved off a few yards before I dared reach for my rod.

"These crafts have a very low profile and can be maneuvered without a sound. In clear water, kayaks can be slowly cruised over areas while anglers look for fish, which is not easy to do when simply wading. You can't cover as much ground."

After publishing an article about kayak fishing in an outdoors publication, I conducted a kayak stealth test (albeit very unscientific). My friend Bill Killian and I took out a fiberglass bass boat and a small kayak. I also took along scuba gear.

I dropped down to the bottom in 5-feet of water using the scuba gear and got Bill to pass over my position in the fiberglass boat using a trolling motor. I could easily hear him passing overhead. Then he

Wade-fishing allows the fly-fisherman to creep up on his prey. A kayak will allow him to glide up even more silently.

repeated the maneuver in the kayak. Although I could see the boat, I could barely hear him paddling.

The next test was for Bill to wade in 3-feet of water on a sandbar a couple of hundred yards away while I rested on the bottom in scuba gear. I told him to move quietly like he would when wade-fishing.

Bottom line: the kayak was the quietest, and the trolling motor was quieter than wading.

Stan Rodgers of Key Largo, Florida, understands this concept as well as anyone. He has been using kayaks to sneak up on snook, tarpon, and permit for years and is still surprised at how closely he can approach fish. "It's just amazing. Once you get into the rhythm of your particular craft, the ability to encounter game fish at point-blank range is mind boggling," he said.

One encounter in particular sticks in his mind: "Permit around the keys can be very, very spooky, and I have found them to be the hardest of all fish to approach. Occasionally, you will get a dumb one that is not paying attention, but most of the time, permit are super-alert. One day, I was out looking for barracuda to catch on a fly rod and noticed a permit in about two feet of water. It was a really big fish. I eventually made my way over close enough to make a cast with my Clouser Minnow, all the while I never took my eye off of that fish. After making two unsuccessful casts, something caught my eye and there was an even bigger permit feeding right next to my boat about two feet away. Now here's the amazing part: I was actually able to move back a few feet and cast over to that fish and catch it. If I wasn't a true believer in kayaks then, I was after that encounter."

Now that we've established that kayaks equal stealth, let's take a look at the physical requirements for using a kayak.

You don't want to be totally out of shape, as it always helps to be in shape when doing anything. Actually, I would say that any person in average physical condition is a good candidate to learn kayaking. Sure, it can be strenuous. If you like to mix in a little exercise with your fishing, then all the more reason to take up the paddle. Actually, fishing out of a kayak is probably less strenuous than wading on mucky bottoms. If you are presently out of shape or restrained in some way, there is still plenty of fun to be had. To mix a metaphor, I liken it to riding a bicycle: paddle or peddle at your own speed.

Another issue kayaks address is fishing access. Many coastal anglers don't own boats, and most of the time that's due to finances. A new bay boat can cost nearly $20,000 while a kayak can cost under $1,000. Sure, a bay boat will take an angler greater distances in a short time, but a kayak allows access to places a motor boat simply cannot go. It takes only a few inches of water for a kayak to remain afloat. Some of the best places to kayak are tidal lakes, tidal flats, and remote salt marsh lakes. The kayak opens a whole new world to the fisherman whose bay rig needs one to two feet of water to navigate safely and comfortably. Some salt marsh lakes are 6-inches deep in spots, but they hold lots of fish. Many of these areas are located a short distance from bank fishing locations where a quick trip in a kayak could put the angler into an area no one else can access.

Kayaks certainly aren't the be-all-end-all of coastal fishing. Learning to fish out of them can take some serious adjustments, and they certainly don't have as much space as conventional boats. Nonetheless, for anglers who want to try something a little different, kayaks are the answer to a lot of questions.

chapter eight

Jetties:
Hard rock trout cafes

Jetties are my favorite places to catch speckled trout. These rock structures prevent sand washing into boat channels between ship channels and the Gulf of Mexico. The water around these structures probably holds more fish per acre than any other.

The general rule among dedicated jetty fishermen is that anything caught in the bays can be caught in greater numbers and often in larger size at the jetties. This is especially true for speckled trout.

Finding a good jetty is simple since all of them are productive. Some of my favorites are Sabine, Cameron, Galveston, South Pass, and Port Aransas. The Surfside jetties near Freeport also deserve a mention since they allow walk-in access.

ASSESSING JETTIES

All Gulf Coast jetties hold good numbers of trout, but it takes know-how to have good trips most of the time. Trout fishing at the jetties is a very misunderstood practice. By that, I mean first-time jetty fishermen tend to think trout are present at every rock along the jetty wall, but nothing could be farther from the truth. Trout often bond to specific pieces of the structure. This is why a good depthfinder is important. Many times the fish will be tightly stacked together. Last year, while fishing the Galveston jetties, the only place we could get a trout to bite was between two large rocks. If we threw anywhere else, we caught gafftopsail catfish.

Another reason for electronics is that it is important to look for subtle structure. When looking at a jetty, it is obvious there is a lot of structure around the top, but there is plenty more around the base of the structure. Think of the visible portion as the proverbial "tip of the iceberg." The visible rocks are the top of a pyramid-shaped stack that is three times as wide at the base. A jetty 10 feet wide at the top is 30 feet wide at the bottom.

Trout often hover around one small piece of rock. At the Sabine jetties, they gather around a small boat wreck that sits about 10 feet away from the jetty. Bass fishermen often talk about fishing the "secondary points" of a reservoir. They are talking about fishing a point that is not visible to the naked eye but are obvious underwater. I think of these small pieces of structure as "secondary points" and look for them first. If no trout are there, I can back off and fish the "main point," which would be the visible and obvious parts of the system.

TACKLE & BAITS

Fishing jetties calls for very little special tackle. I prefer to use a medium-heavy popping rod, like my 7 1/2-foot Shakespeare Ugly Stik or All Star popping rods. Any good casting reel will get the job done. The most important tackle considerations are lures and baits. In soft plastics, I like the Culprit Rip Tide shrimp tails, Berkley Power Mullet, DOA Shrimp, and any large-bodied luminescent-colored grub. It is important to have a range of jighead selections. I carry everything from 1/8-ounce to 5/8-ounce. Current can be killer around jetties, and when trout are belly-to-the-bottom, the 1/8-ounce is not going to get the lure where it needs to go.

Sometimes the boat or safety cut in the jetty wall holds lots of fish. The tidal flow can be incredibly strong in these spots since a huge amount of water is trying to move through a small space in a short time. Trout will lie on the edge of this flow to mop up on baitfishes that move through. By using a troll motor and working through these spots with a Rat-L-Trap or a gold spoon, anglers can target these fish with

Jetty rocks are the author's favorite places to catch trout.

relative ease. Another good way to target these trout is to throw a silver spoon up against the rocks and let it flutter down. Some friends of mine have used the Charlie Slab, which is popular with freshwater

Live bait tends to work best when fishing the rocks.

white bass fishermen, to catch trout off the Louisiana coast. They like the white and yellow version.

My favorite bait for jetties is live shrimp. Fished on a free-line or popping cork, it is hard to beat and probably catches more jetty trout than all other baits and lures combined.

Croaker is also an excellent choice for jetty fishing and can be fished on a free-line, cork, or on the bottom. Sometimes croaker is hard to get from bait shops, so bring a rod and reel rigged with a double leader, some small hooks, and dead shrimp. Jetties are usually loaded with croaker, so you can catch bait as you are fishing. Sometimes the croaker you catch will be rather large, but do not be afraid to use them. Back in the 1960s, my father caught 9-pound trout on foot long croakers at the Cameron jetties.

Capt. David Dillman, of Speck-Tacular Trout Adventures, frequents the jetties at Galveston and believes live bait is the best bet for summer fishing: "In the fall, trout at the jetties will hammer a lure, but during spring and summer, they much prefer the real thing. I've had tremendous success on big trout using live bait at these jetties."

Croaker and shrimp are the main choice of speck hunters in many areas, but Dillman prefers piggy perch: "There are not very many people using piggies, but they are fairly easy to catch on your own. Croaker is a good trout bait, but the big trout seem to like the piggies. Piggies, for some reason, seem to get the bigger fish on the jetties out here. I'll use them up to about the size of my palm or a little bigger and catch trout all day. The most important thing to remember is that you have to fish way up close to the rocks, or you're missing out. The rocks are what hold the fish to the area."

For those who prefer artificials, a DOA Shrimp fished under a popping cork can be a deadly combination. For the past two years, I've been using the 1/4-ounce clear shrimp with a chartreuse tail for sandy-green water and the glow version when the water is off-colored. Another good method for the DOA shrimp is to rig it with a 1/8-ounce split shot weight fixed about a foot above the bait and let it flow with the current parallel to the jetty wall. On a strong tide, this technique locates fish quickly. Remember that the outside (Gulf) side of a jetty is best on an incoming tide, and the inside (channel) side is best on an outgoing tide.

PRE DAWN ACTION

The best jetty fishermen I know are two guys who would probably lynch me if I mentioned their name in relation to the tactic I am about

Anchor at the jetties before dawn, and your chances of boating specks are greatly improved.

to describe. These two fellows anchor up at the jetties a good hour and a half before dawn and fish with topwater plugs. They do this on calm, summer days when the water is gently beating against the rocks on the extreme southern ends of the jetties. These guys routinely limit out on 4 to 7-pound trout.

Catching trout on topwater plugs is fun enough, but doing it at the jetties at night is intense beyond description. The secretive duo likes to fish with large topwater plugs like the Super Spook and Top Dog. The Rattlin' Chug Bug is another I have heard mentioned in their circle. If I could force myself to get out of bed at 2 a.m., I would try this method myself, but that is a tall order for me, especially when I know I can get trout on the tide movements all day.

Winter Jetty Trout

Most anglers fish jetties during spring, summer, and fall, leaving the winter season for self-proclaimed jetty junkies like me to pursue not-so-glamorous species like sheepshead and black drum. There are trout at the jetties in winter too, but they act differently than they do the rest of the year. The most glaring difference is they do not feed aggressively, and an angler must work to find them. I am relatively new to winter jetty fishing but have found the fish congregate around the deeper holes and hold belly-to-the-bottom or suspend about 75 percent down the water column. These fish bite very discreetly. In my experience, I have found it is sometimes easier to detect strikes by sight rather than feel. Last winter, I caught some jetty trout by fishing with big shad hooked onto a 1/2-ounce jighead and suspended about six inches above the bottom. When the line wiggled or began to move, I set the hook hard. This type of fishing commands strict attention, but it usually pays off.

The best rod for this technique depends on how sporting you feel. The chances of landing a big trout on an ultralight rig are slim and none. These fish are hard, consistent fighters that do not give up easy, so I would leave the crappie rigs at home. A good setup would be a 6- to 7-foot medium-heavy action rod with a bait-casting reel. I use an Abu Garcia Ambassadeur 5000 on an All Star graphite rod. Any sturdy redfish or bass rig will suffice, though.

Line selection depends on how many fish you want to actually land. A strong 15-pound-test would be a minimum in most cases since the fish congregate around line-abrading structure. Since casting is not always necessary, you can easily go with line in the 20-pound-test class with a heavy steel leader. Some of the braided lines are excellent due to their extreme sensitivity. I have used Berkley Fireline with great success.

Sometimes fishing on the bottom is best and I use what I call my "jetty sheepshead rig." It consists of a 1-ounce egg sinker rigged above a bead above a swivel and attached to 2-feet of a light steel leader and a No. 2 hook. This rig is easy to set up. All you have to do is put the sinker on your line and then the bead. Tie a swivel to the end of the line to stop the bead and sinker from sliding off. Then tie a leader to the swivel and the hook to the leader.

JETTY SAFETY

Since jetties are part ship channel and part Gulf of Mexico, safety precautions are a major part of any fishing trip. The first hazard to watch out for is large waves caused by oil tankers and discourteous crew boats. The latter are not supposed to run fast in ship channels but often do, spawning waves larger than big tankers. I have given more than a few of them "sign language" over the years.

Current is something to watch for around jetties because it can be incredibly strong and equally dangerous. Rip currents, sometimes mistakenly called "rip tides" or "undertows" (they have nothing to do with tides and do not pull people under), are the most threatening natural hazard along the coast, pulling incautious swimmers and other victims away from the beach out to sea. A rip current is a seaward-moving current that circulates water back to sea after it is pushed ashore by waves. Each wave accumulates water on shore creating seaward pressure. This pressure is released in an area with the least amount of resistance, which is usually the deepest point along the ocean floor. Rip currents also exist in areas where wave strength is weakened by objects such as jetties, piers, natural reefs, and even large groups of bathers. Rip currents often look like muddy rivers flowing away from shore. The United States Lifesaving Association has found that 80 percent of the rescues affected by ocean lifeguards involve people caught in rip currents.

Chapter 8 | Jetties

Pitching live bait or soft plastics against the wall at virtually any of the jetty systems on the Texas coast is a great way to hang into a monster trout.

I've seen lots of rip currents at the Sabine, Cameron, and Galveston Jetties. The major danger posed by these currents is to small craft, particularly aluminum boats like the one I frequently fish from. If your motor dies, for example, you could be swept onto the rocks or sucked out toward the Gulf into what I call "the gauntlet"— the first couple of miles of Gulf out of the mouth of a jetty. The seas in these areas are rough and dangerous for a small boat and to be avoided at all costs.

Proper anchoring at jetties is very important for safety as well as proper fishing. Be prepared to lose anchors. I would bet there are 10,000 anchors lodged along the Galveston jetties alone. Throwing a hunk of lead into a mountain of jagged granite is a recipe for irretrievable snagging. Anyway, follow these simple tips for good, safe jetty anchoring and you might even avoid losing yours.

- Use lots of rope. About 125 feet should be enough.
- Between the rope and anchor, there should be at least 5-feet of

heavy chain. This helps keep the anchor on the bottom.

- Never shut off the engine while anchoring. You could easily drift into the rocks and cause severe damage to your boat, another craft, or yourself.

- Always be mindful of where your boat is positioned in relation to the rocks. Tides can change quickly, and fiberglass doesn't do well again granite. Give yourself some distance from the rocks when anchoring.

- Anchor upcurrent from the intended fishing hole, then drift over the spot and tie off.

- Use an anchor designed for jetties. I've been using an anchor called the Mighty-Mite and have found it an ideal jetty anchor. It has specially designed prongs that provide a steady grip but can be dislodged from just about any rocky crevice.

- Night fishing with floating or submersible green lights is a highly effective way of landing trout and is becoming increasingly popular. Be careful, though. Navigating jetties at night is quite dangerous. Anchor on the Gulf side if the seas are calm enough. A friend of mine ended up getting his aluminum boat thrown on top of the Sabine jetties by a wave from a passing oil tanker. His boat was destroyed, and he and his fishing partner sustained minor injuries. It could have been worse—a *lot* worse.

WATCH OUT FOR THE LAW

Anglers fishing the nearshore Gulf of Mexico east of the Sabine jetties should beware: waters generally assumed under federal control may not be. According to Louisiana Department of Wildlife and Fisheries game warden Capt. Malcolm Hebert, Louisiana has authority over waters extending three miles past the Sabine Jetties: "Following a line straight from the end of the east jetty out three miles is Louisiana water. That is farther than the standard three-mile state water limit for all other areas of the Louisiana coast. This extension of Louisiana State territory comes back to the east and forms a semi-circle that hits the standard 3-mile line of state water boundary."

Louisiana, like all Gulf states besides Florida and Texas, control their coastal waters 3-miles out. Anything beyond that is under federal control. In other words, a Louisiana license is not necessary for local anglers to fish off the Louisiana coast if they are beyond the 3-mile boundary—except, that is, in the Sabine Pass area. When asked where this semi-circle ends, Hebert said he wasn't sure, but it includes some of the rigs off the Louisiana jetties: "Some of those rigs that Texas anglers like to fish for trout and other species are part of this extension. We wrote citations there last year and had wardens waiting on the rig for them."

According to Hebert, technically, Louisiana wardens are supposed to haul anglers caught fishing in their waters without a license to jail, but they've worked out a compromise: "We are taking their rods and reels and bringing them back to Lake Charles. They either pay their fine or lose their equipment. Right now we have over 100 rods and reels from anglers who broke the law over here."

Where this authority to extend state water boundaries came from is a mystery; Louisiana State officials will not answer that question.

Anglers fishing east of the Louisiana jetty should exercise caution if they do not have a Louisiana license. I personally broke the law several times without knowing it, and, according to Hebert, I wasn't the only one. I was just a lucky one that did not get ticketed.

OTHER SPECIES

Yes, this is a trout book, but jetties are fun to fish partly because an angler never knows what he's going to catch. Besides specks, there are redfish, jack crevalle, stingrays, sharks, Spanish mackerel, sheepshead, and a host of other species. Sometimes you hook into something and think it is the state record trout or a submarine-sized red that turns out to be a big jack—or just about anything else that swims the salt, including pelagic species.

On one of my first jetty trips, I caught two heavy blacktip sharks and a 70-pound stingray. By the time that beast was boated, I was almost too tired to fish for trout, but it did not really matter. I was hooked for life. On that note, anglers who have never tried jetty fishing should be aware that it is addictive. Remember, the rule is that anything that can be caught in the bay is bigger at the jetties.

If that is not a sweet enticement, I do not know what is.

chapter nine

Short rig savvy:
Striking trout where they drilled for oil

There was barely a ripple on the surface of the blue-green tinted Gulf of Mexico. My fishing partner, Bill Killian, and I originally intended to do some trout fishing at the Sabine jetties, but the lure of calm and clear Gulf waters was too strong. We changed our course to one of the short rigs (nearshore oil or natural gas platforms).

Three miles due south of the Sabine jetties sits a small, unmanned rig most anglers ignore. It looks too close to shore to harbor any good "offshore" action for species like red snapper. We, however, were looking for "inshore" species.

After tying off to the rig, we grabbed our medium-heavy action popping rods rigged with 1/2-ounce jighead and a chartreuse-colored Culprit shrimp tails and went to work. We cast to the platform and let the lure sweep back toward the boat as it made its way through the current toward the muddy bottom.

Wham! I got hooked up.

Saltwater Strategies Book Series: **TEXAS TROUT TACTICS**

"Short rigs" is a term used for nearshore oil and gas platforms in the Gulf of Mexico. On the Upper Texas Coast and in Louisiana, these areas are considered one of the top areas for catching big trout in the summer.

Wham! Bill got hooked up.

We were both battling big speckled trout, which is exactly what we were after. Two more casts equaled two more fish and proved we made the right move. Over the next hour, we would catch near-limits of quality speckled trout while boat after boat passed us up to head for deeper waters. Reports from the jetties that day ranged from fair to abysmal. Such are the benefits of short rig speckled trout fishing.

Surf-fishermen know that Gulf waters harbor plenty of quality trout, but relatively few realize the tremendous fishing opportunities that exist beyond the sandbars at the short rigs. Over the past few years, I have caught many speckled trout by fishing at the short rigs of Sabine Pass, Cameron, Bolivar, and the Chandeleur Islands. I will be the first to tell you this kind of fishing has no guarantees. It can be extremely slow, but it can also be the best thing going. You just have to decide if you are willing to invest a little extra time to try something different.

STRUCTURE AND LOCATION

Perhaps the most important tool for catching short rig specks is a fish finder. Many times these fish will be bunched tightly together. While fishing with Capt. Daniel Pyle of State Line Guide Service, we found trout stacked in a 10 square-foot area. At least that was our best guess at its size. When we cast beyond this spot, we wouldn't get a hit. Cast into it, and the lure never had a chance to hit the bottom. Old-timers tell me trout stack in such tight groups because of the presence of sharks. They say it is the old safety in numbers thing. I do not doubt this is true since it is obvious speckled trout are prey for sharks. Anyone who has ever spent much time fishing the surf has probably had a shark tug on their stringer and maybe rob a trout or two. Some of us have been fighting trout only to reel in half a fish—the other half in the belly of a shark.

Another reason for the importance of electronics is the need to look for subtle structure around the rigs. When looking at a rig, it is obvious there is a lot of structure around the legs and support bars, and trout are often caught there. There is usually plenty more structure and trout around the perimeter of the rig. Rigs have cables, underwater support bars, capped off well heads, and other fixtures. Many times trout will hover around one small piece of this structure. At one of my favorite rigs, they gather around a small boat wreck that sits about 10 yards away. The first time I fished this rig, I was perturbed that the guy across from me was catching trout after trout while I only managed to puck up the odd straggler. I was using the same bait and retrieve and fishing less than 30 yards away. When the guy caught his limit and left, I moved to his spot and immediately started catching fish.

I know one angler who routinely fishes a capped-off well head a few miles southeast of the Galveston jetties. The only structure there is the well head itself, which sits under 35 feet of water; it harbors many trout at certain times.

Bass fishermen often talk about fishing the "secondary points" of a reservoir. They are talking about fishing the point that is not visible to the naked eye but obvious underwater. I think of these small pieces of structure as "secondary points" and look for them first. If there are not trout there, I can always back off and fish the "main point," which would be the visible and obvious parts of a rig.

Tackle and Bait Selection

Lure selection is the most important tackle consideration for fishing short rigs. In soft plastics, I like the Culprit Rip Tide shrimp tails, Berkley Power Mullet, DOA shrimp, and any large-bodied luminescent-colored grub. It is important to have a wide range of jighead selections. I carry everything from 1/8- to 5/8-ounce so I can adjust for any current scenario.

Jigging spoons can be killer at the rigs. The Charlie Slab, mentioned in the chapter on jetty fishing, works well. At the suggestion of Charles Spell, former owner of Gulf Coast Tackle in Beaumont, Texas, I started using the Hoginar. It looks like a useless scrap of lead, but it is a tremendous lure for catching specks in deep water.

Picking a good line for the short rigs is not quite so pat. Opinions are as varied as the situations an angler will find himself in out there. I have tested out a few different brands and have a couple of favorite for this application.

I took out some of the P-Line CXX X-tra Strong fishing line to the oil rigs out of Galveston in the spring of 2002. I had fished with the original P-line, a super strong monofilament, in Venezuela in December 1999 and found it great for yanking big peacock bass out of the brushy, flooded rainforest surrounding Lake Guri. I wanted to see if the CXX X-TRA Strong would yield the same results in the Gulf, and it did. Bill Killian and I were free-lining live shrimp around some platforms and catching big sheepshead and southern pompano. The fish held tight to the platform legs, so we had to tighten down our drags and pull the fish away before they hit the sharp barnacles. We found no problem with cranking down the drag to nearly nothing on the 17-pound-test and pulling the hard-fighting fish into the boat. In fact, one of the pompano brushed the line against the platform legs, but it did not break. That says a lot for its abrasion resistance.

With smaller fish like sheepshead or even red snapper, offshore anglers walk a fine line (no pun intended). Braided lines give better sensitivity than any mono, but the lack of stretch can cause problems in deep water on trout, which have soft mouths. Regular mono stretches too much for my tastes, and does not have the abrasion resistance to get the job done.

Another excellent choice is Excalibur line. This stuff has incredible abrasion resistance. While using 14-pound Excalibur, I hooked a Spanish mackerel at an oil platform near Sabine Pass. The fish wrapped around one of the barnacle-encrusted pilings but did not cut the line.

SPECIAL TACTICS FOR SUSPENDED FISH

Sometimes short rig trout will suspend midway in the water column. This can mean they are holding 20 feet down in 40 feet of water. This calls for special tactics. A good option is to locate these fish and anchor a good 20 yards upcurrent. Let your bait slowly sink toward the target depth and drift into the fish. Live bait like croaker or piggy perch is an excellent choice for this method. These suspended fish often act very finicky and sometimes will not take standard offerings. By fishing live bait on a Kahle hook with a couple of split shots rigged about a foot above it, you can often entice these fish into biting.

Live bait, unfortunately, ends up catching lots of unwelcome (depending on the angler) species. Many of them have a mouthful of teeth that can cut a line in a heartbeat. Some anglers use thin steel leaders to avoid getting cut off by Spanish mackerel and small sharks. If you get a big shark, it is not going to matter; they are going to break off with trout tackle. The leader offers some additional protection from the pilings of the rigs.

Florida live baiters are beginning to use circle hooks, which I have advocated for trout fishing for quite some time. This allows the fish to hook themselves and helps ensure live release. Most of the time, the circle hook lodges in the corner of the trout's mouth. The only problem is that it is hard to find circle hooks small enough for trout. A good alternative is the Daiichi Tru-Turn hook. It is sort of a circle/j-style hybrid that works like a circle hook.

If the current is slack, slow-sinking jerkbaits like Bass Assassins or Slimy Slugs are good choices. Something like the hard plastic, slow-sinking MirrOlure 2000 is also great for this application. It would also better survive the strike of big redfish, which often strike at slow-sinking lures at the rigs.

Kamikaze Fishing

I coined the term "kamikaze fishing" when Dean Dyson and I caught some nice trout inside of a natural gas platform while fishing

The short rigs are loaded with trout and sharks. It is not rare to be fighting a big speck and a shark comes out from the structure to take advantage of the situation.

from my 16-foot Grumman aluminum boat. The rig was very close to shore and the seas as calm as you could ask for. We were not catching fish outside of the platform, but something was tearing up bait inside the rig. We decided to move in. The rig had one side completely open, so we tied the boat off to a pole in the middle of the platform and proceeded to annihilate the fish. Dean ended up catching a 27-incher that day.

Most rigs do not offer access to their insides, and I do not recommend doing what we did, but I do advise fishing inside a rig by other means. If there is an opening, make exploratory casts inside to see what

Specks aren't the only game fish caught at the rigs. Here Chester Moore poses with a big redfish.

you can stir up. These spots can be sanctuaries for big trout.

This brings up the important point of boat positioning. At rigs, an angler has three choices: anchor, tie up, or fish around it with a trolling motor. Anchoring and tying up to the rig puts you at the mercy of the currents, which can be brutal. You have to fish at a position where the current drifts you away from the rig, unless you're in a small craft and are willing to do goofy things like Dean and I did that day.

Using trolling motors is tough with all of the wave action and current, but if you have one strong enough, I suggest you bring it along. It could help put you in the exact spot, and in the world of short rig fishing that's of utmost importance.

Rogue Trout

It was a sight I will not soon forget: My wife, Lisa, and I were tied off to an oil platform 7-miles off the coast of High Island, Texas, when a large school of spadefish moved in. We caught a fair number of fish and were enjoying a beautiful albeit hot day on the water. Seeing the spadefish reminded me it would be cooler in the water. I always carry snorkeling gear and my Sea & Sea MX-10 underwater camera on offshore trips. The water was smooth and clear, and the chance to photograph the pretty spadefish was too tempting to resist.

Each time I dove down to photograph the spades, I could see a silver form about halfway down the platform leg. Curiosity finally got the best of me. I took a deep breath and went down to see what it was. As I descended, the silver form took the shape of a fish. At first, I thought it might be a small kingfish or wayward barracuda, but as I got closer, I realized it was a speckled trout— a huge one.

It took a second for the magnitude of what I was looking at to set in. As I started to run out of air and ascend, the fish swam right next to the platform leg. It was nearly as long as the legs were wide. If this

The short rigs, with ideal structure and low fishing pressure, offer great opportunities for big trout catches.

fish was not 3 feet long and 13 or 14 pounds, it was mighty close. I was so astonished I forgot to photograph it—big time screw-up. When I surfaced, Lisa asked if I had seen a big shark or something. She said I was as white as a sheet.

I will spare you the depressing details of the rest of the trip, but I will say an impending thunderstorm forced us to return to the ramp rather than chunk lures at the magnificent fish. I will never forget that experience.

The trout Mike Daleo saw at some rigs in Southwest Louisiana will never leave his mind either: "I saw this good-sized blue crab detach from one of the platform legs and start swimming in the open water. Pretty soon, this trout comes up and inhales the crab. I would like to reiterate this was no small crab. That trout was the biggest I have ever seen, absolutely huge."

The rigs Daleo likes to fish are legendary among anglers in the Sabine Pass and Cameron area. While they have never produced a legitimate giant, scores of fish up to 9 pounds have been caught, and many tales of monster rogue trout circulate around bait shops and boat docks in the area.

I believe state record-class fish can be found at the short rigs along the Texas, Louisiana, and Mississippi coasts. I have seen legitimate monster-caliber fish and know other anglers who have had similar encounters. If you think about it, these areas are perfect habitat for trophy-sized fish. Compared to bay systems, they are lightly pressured and offer a big fish plenty of cover and escape routes. Landing a small fish around rigs can be a challenge at times due to all of the pipes, cables, and other obstructions. Landing big ones on trout tackle can be downright difficult. If I were a trout, I would live on a short rig.

WHEN AND WHERE TO FISH

Short rig trout fishing can be good any time from late spring on through October. The best fishing is usually during the summer months. May through mid-September are the peak times, and these months usually give up the best fishing conditions.

The first thing to consider is wind. If the wind is strong and seas are even a little rough, you would be better off staying in the bay or the protection of the jetties. A good calm day is not only safer to fish but easier as well. It is virtually impossible to get good lure action when winds are howling and the seas are threatening to throw your boat into the rig.

Water clarity is something else to consider. The general rule is that if the water is ranging anywhere in the green or blue, the shore rigs are worth checking out.

Where to fish is basically anywhere from Alabama to Texas where rigs sit within a few miles of shore. The hottest spots are in the area of the Chandeleur Islands, the coast of Cameron, Louisiana, and between Sabine Pass and Galveston, Texas. There are literally hundreds of rigs in these areas and potentially thousands of fish to encounter.

chapter ten

Going to the bank:
Cashing in on surf, pier, and shoreline fishing

Owning a boat is not a requirement of catching good numbers of speckled trout. There are hundreds of miles of beach, bay shoreline, and many fishing piers that allow bank fishermen to access trout. There are even times when the presumed disadvantage of not having a boat gives the angler a real edge.

FISHING THE SURF

Summertime is the best for catching trout in the surf. Large schools of these voracious predators chase baitfishes between the sandbars. The problem for most first-time surf-fishermen is learning where to fish. To a novice, one stretch of surf looks like any other, but to the experienced angler, there are dramatic differences. For starters, there is structure.

Let's start with points. Points are parts of the shore that extend into the water. They can be small or quite large. The most common

Saltwater Strategies Book Series: **TEXAS TROUT TACTICS**

The surf offers boatless anglers a chance to log some serious trout time.

configuration extends out at right angles to the beach. Occasionally, the beach will turn and a "point" will look more like a "bend" but they are essentially the same. Smaller points are less noticeable but still detectable by the current rips they produce, or by the way waves break over them.

Most anglers choose to fish at the tip of the point because that is where the most baitfishes congregate, and, thus, predators show up. Going back to the beach, the sides of a sandy point are good, especially in the "pocket"—a depression scooped out by crashing waves and current.

Bowls are another type of surf structure. Bowls typically indent into the shore and form between two points. Many bowls form in what is called a "teacup" configuration. If you ever hear someone say they caught fish in the "teacup," they are not speaking in code but talking about a bowl in the surf. Some bowls are subtler and visible only when tides are low, which brings up a good point. During winter, when low tides are common after northers pass through, bring a GPS unit and camera. Photograph the structure and mark its location with the GPS. This will give you a huge advantage over other anglers and help you eliminate a lot of infertile surf when the fish are biting.

Fishing a bowl involves working along the "rims" with special emphasis on the upper rims or spots where the bowl transitions to a point. The center of a bowl can be great too because these are often the deepest points. In shallow surf, sudden depth usually means fish.

Troughs or "guts" are the long depressions or ditches running parallel to the shoreline and sandbars. Surf-fishermen often talk about fishing "between the sandbars," which refers to fishing the troughs in the surf. The sandbars can be the bottom between the troughs or an actual "bar" formed by current.

In deeper water, trout feed along the sloping sides of a trough, but in deeper surf, they feed in the center. Old-timers say that trout gravitate toward the sharpest edge of the trough.

Sandbars, as explained earlier, parallel the shore for great distances. For surf-fishing for sharks, bull redfish, and other big predators, it is important to fish the outer sandbar, which is why anglers wade out to their shoulders and throw long surf rods. For trout, the inner bars can be just as productive.

Most surf-fishing experts agree that fish feed along the sloping outer or front side of the bar. They gravitate toward where the sloping front of the bar ends.

Learning to identify this "surf structure" allows you to fish the surf with less guesswork. Trout in the surf are famous for paralleling the beach and making long runs, and this is when knowing what structure is most effective becomes very important. Instead of running down the beach fishing everything, try the points or troughs or whatever structure has been productive recently; surf-fishing has a way of falling into a pattern when the weather gets stable.

Case study: Constance Beach

If there has ever been a "perfect" piece of surf for trout fishing, it is Constance Beach in Southwest Louisiana. I would like to dedicate a major portion of this chapter to experiences other anglers and I have had at Constance Beach. The rock jetties that line the beach will be a big part of beach management in the future in Texas and elsewhere along the Gulf Coast. This is a section for the future or present if you live in an area with a surf line like Constance Beach.

The system of rocks and pilings that parallel the beach was put there to protect the fragile beach and adjacent wetland habitats from the awesome power of erosion. A combination of hurricanes and a

Chapter 10 | Going to the bank

Sand, surf and specks... a combustible angling formula.

constant pounding from Gulf winds have left the fragile ecosystem severely bruised, so the government stepped in to halt the destruction.

Ask any of the dedicated anglers who fish these waters why the rocks were put there, and you may get a different answer: "Them is fishing rocks. They put them there to improve the fishing down here, and it worked," said Mack Thibodeaux.

Thibodeaux, a Cameron Parish resident who frequents the area, likes to joke about the purpose of the rock jetties that lie just 75 yards off the Constance Beach surf, but he is serious about their effect on the area's fishing. Like bees to honey, the rocks have attracted game fish to this little corner of coastal Louisiana in a big way: "This has always been good surf to fish, but over the last two years, we have really seen that the rocks have improved our fishing, especially for the trout, and they have made fishing the surf a whole lot easier too."

Thibodeaux is one of many who pursue speckled trout around the Constance Beach rocks. Being a practical angler, he realizes that summertime surf specks aren't known for their size, but he is familiar enough with this unique beach system to know that it can be a real sleeper for trophy fish at times: "Most of the fish that I catch out here are just good solid fish in the 3- to 4-pound range, but I would be lying if I told you that I haven't caught trout up to 8 pounds here."

Thibodeaux is a firm believer in the "early bird gets the worm" theory. He likes to get to the beach well before sunrise to cash in on the shallow bite. He also contends that this is the best time to catch the big trout: "About an hour or so before day breaks, the trout will be between the surf and the rocks. That water is only about 2 1/2 to 3 feet deep, so it's best to just stand on the bank and cast in to not spook the fish away. I have caught most of my big trout before sunrise. I guess they're kind of like a trophy whitetail buck, they prowl the most when people prowl the least."

In the bait department, Thibodeaux starts with two different rods. He always throws out one with a live finger mullet or pogey rigged under a popping cork and sets it in a rod holder. Then he works over the surf with a DOA Bait Buster: "Live bait is always a good choice before sunup, and that Bait Buster is a real obtrusive bait. It is big and gaudy and disturbs a lot of water. When it is dark, I like a bait like that to get the trout's attention. It's not unusual for me to have fish on both rods when I fish like that."

As the morning wears on, Thibodeaux usually puts away his live bait and walks out in the surf to work around the rocks. Sunrise pushes the fish farther out, and the inner edge of the rocks is a great place to start. If he doesn't find fish here, he climbs on top of the rocks and shoots out toward the second sand bar to jig the Bait Buster across the bottom. Once the sun gets up high, Thibodeaux changes baits—he likes to feed the trout with a spoon: "I don't care what you say, on a good, sunny day, a silver spoon is just about impossible to beat when it comes to trout fishing. Just throw that sucker out there and retrieve it kind of slow and there's no telling what you are gonna catch."

Thibodeaux looks for feeding fish and tries to cast a few feet past them. He also jigs the spoon straight down from the rocks. He said that is a good way to lose your spoon, but it also produces some trout: "I rarely have a day out there when I don't catch several fish straight down from the rocks while standing on top of them."

The only other bait Thibodeaux carries with him are a few Rattlin' Chug Bugs. After he has caught enough fish to eat, he ties one on just for the fun of it: "I like my spoons and Bait Busters, but topwaters are awful fun to fish."

Joe Persohn is also a fan of the Constance rocks. He likes to fish them from a boat so he can easily move from place to place following the major schools of fish: "Those rocks can be hot as a firecracker for trout. I've been there several times when I have limited before 7:30 a.m. Now, that is what I call fishing."

Persohn said that by boat, your best bet is to fish the surf on a high tide and cast down parallel to the rocks. Since many of the trout hug the rocks, this technique is most productive. In the bait department,

Saltwater Strategies Book Series: **TEXAS TROUT TACTICS**

Fishing the surf is exhilerating, but also dangerous.

Persohn sticks with soft plastics: "I have been fishing a Charlie's worm. They're a paddle-tailed worm and scented. Open that pack up and it smells like a watermelon rind, kind of like a good trout slick. I fish them on a 3/8-ounce jighead and throw them straight down those rocks. I'm telling you, this is a trout killer."

The U.S. Army Corps of Engineers is talking about putting up similar structures all along the Gulf coast. Pray they do, because they are truly trout magnets.

Extreme Surf-fishing

Some time back, I received an e-mail from an angler who wanted to share his unique and quite extreme method for catching big trout in the surf. He fishes with a surf rod like the kind used for bull redfish and sharks, but he fishes with big live croaker. He throws the croaker out between the last two sandbars and lets it sit until a big sow trout engulfs it. He said he has caught trout up to 8 pounds doing this and the only problem is that it's slow and he tends to catch a lot of big redfish. Nice problem to have.

Surf Safety

There are some unique safety factors when surf-fishing. Sharks are one of them. There are big sharks in the surf and, for the most part, they won't bother you, but that doesn't mean you should invite trouble. Use a long stringer that extends a good 10 feet. Pulling strung fish close behind you is inviting trouble.

Another monster that inhabits the surf is the stingray, which can pose problems for surf-fisherman and beach-goers alike. To guard against stingray encounters, it is best that waders shuffle their feet in the surf. Stepping on a ray is a sure-fire way to get hurt, whereas shuffling one's feet can alarm the fish so that it moves away.

Follow these tips and safety procedures and you should be on your way to mastering the art of surf-fishing.

PIER-FISHING

Pier-fishing has always fascinated me. Maybe it was because while growing up, we never had enough money to afford a boat to fish in the

Piers offer massive structure to attract bait and trout.

Chapter 10 | Going to the bank

Gulf, but we could scrape up enough to hit the piers at Bolivar Peninsula and Galveston.

Piers may be the best things going for land-bound anglers for two reasons: structure and lighting.

We have already covered how important finding structure is in the surf. Piers provide a gigantic piece of structure attractive to baitfish and trout. Many piers also provide lights at night and this draws in trout like a moth to flame.

Anglers typically fish with live bait, such as shrimp under a popping cork, around the lights. Some throw tandem Speck Rigs or glow-colored soft plastic shrimp tails. Watching the trout school around the lights is quite exciting, and occasionally getting a chance to view the fish hitting a bait in the clear, lighted surf is doubly exciting. Where to position oneself on a pier is a tough call because the trout could be anywhere. In my experience, it is best to arrive early and set up close to where the veteran pier-fishermen set up. They usually know the best areas. Tide tables are also important to watch. A super-high tide will push the trout closer to shore while a low tide pushes them out deeper. This is an issue of common sense when you get down to it.

Do not overlook daytime fishing from piers. Terry Harris, who owned Meacom's Pier for many years, told me of catching huge trout on topwaters from his pier on calm mornings when most anglers had already headed home.

Pier fishing can get confusing and hectic when the trout are running thick because outdoor writers like me put out good reports, and the public responds. Be prepared to fish arm-to-arm with other anglers when the fishing is good.

I have come up with a checklist of items and skills a newcomer to pier-fishing might need. These are the basics, and things I consider essential. In addition to rod, reel, hooks, and baits:

- Get a tide chart and read the chapter in this book on tides. Start fishing before the high tide. High tides typically peak when there is a full or new moon.
- Be patient and stick with your spot. When the fish are not around the pier, there is nothing you can do about it.
- Learn how to tie good knots. Lifting a fish onto a pier with a weak knot is a surefire way to lose it.
- If fishing with live bait, use a good bait bucket. Strong, lively bait will outfish weak stuff every time.
- Bring pliers, because you will catch hardhead catfish. Bringing a good stick to whack them in the head with is not a bad idea either.

OTHER BANKING OPTIONS

Land-bound trout anglers should strongly consider fishing the numerous man-made passes connecting the Gulf and bay systems. Before I was able to afford a boat, I fished areas like Rollover Pass (see Hotspots chapter for details). This area is most well-known for its fall croaker and flounder runs, but speckled trout are often present in large numbers.

Tourists typically go about fishing for trout at these passes by soaking a piece of dead shrimp on the bottom, but more often than not their bait is robbed by notorious bait thieves like hardheads, piggy perch, and grunts. Artificial lures would be the best way to work around the bait thieves if it weren't for the fact that spells of good fishing bring in bunches of anglers. Trying to work a lure from the bank while surrounded by anglers with lines in the water is not only difficult but unsafe. It can lead to tangled lines and maybe a bloody nose for you if you put a hook in someone's kid.

The best bet is to use something live. While live shrimp may fall easily to bait stealers, mud minnows, shad, and croaker have longer

Chapter 10 | Going to the bank

There is plenty of walk-in wading access for trout anglers, especially at the numerous man-made passes between bays and the Gulf.

hook life and will increase your odds of catching reds or trout. Mud minnows are the standard issue in these parts due to the excellent flounder fishing and will more than suffice for trout as noted in the live bait chapter.

Fishing these areas at night with a green fishing light can be highly productive. Rollover Pass is sometimes almost completely green with lights on summer nights.

There are too many good bank fishing spots to feature them all in detail. Consider these "starters" then, after you gain some experience, go looking for others.

chapter eleven

Trout hotspots:
Where the trout are

Finding a place to catch speckled trout on the Gulf Coast is not a challenge. An angler can literally fish anywhere south of the saltwater line and catch quality speckled trout. That does not mean all areas are equal in terms of fishing potential. There are some genuine speckled trout hotspots along the Gulf Coast. Here are some of the best:

LAKE CALCASIEU

Lake Calcasieu has been getting loads of attention over the last couple of years. That is because it has been producing the most consistent trophy trout fishing, and that includes some genuine monsters.

On 10 May 2002, Timothy Mahoney of Lafayette, Louisiana, caught a Calcasieu speck that weighed 11 pounds, 2.5 ounces on certified scales. The fish was 30 1/8-inches long with a 16 7/8-inch girth. He was fishing with guide Steve Bono of Bayou Charter Service.

This monster was caught on a glow/chartreuse Norton Sand Eel, Jr.

fished at a washout on the south end of the lake on a big incoming tide. It is the new Lake Calcasieu record and the third largest trout ever in the Louisiana records books.

Capt. Buddy Oakes, of the Hackberry Rod & Gun Club, said that over the last couple of springs, clients have landed fish topping 9 pounds and numerous specimens between 5 and 8 pounds. "It has been

The marshy shorelines of Lake Calcasieu near Lake Charles, Louisiana, produce some of the most consistent action for speckled trout on the Gulf Coast. It is also considered to be the top destination for trophy-sized fish.

a tremendous past few years for Calcasieu, and the trend seems to be continuing," he said.

Oakes noted that during spring, strong south winds sometimes keep anglers off parts of the lake for a while, and disturb the water quality: "The water gets off-colored because of the strong winds, but we still catch big fish. Things always get really good once the wind lays and the water clears. Locating clear water usually means finding fish."

According to guide Capt. Erik Rue, there are plenty of prime locations for Calcasieu first-timers to try: "There are lots of great places to catch nice trout during summer. Turney's Bay gets really good, although the pattern in summer is live bait, and anglers should expect to catch lots of smaller trout. Turney's Bay is best on a light wind out of the north or the west with an outgoing tide.

"Commissary Point, in the middle of the lake just south of Hebert's Landing, is a good spot to hit after most of the boats have left and the water clears. The key here is bait. It is deeper than much of the lake and always has a steady bait supply and good numbers of fish.

"The best spots for big fish are Lambert's Bayou, Lambert's Bayou Reef, and Grand Bayou good spots to catch big fish on live bait or throw topwaters. Lots of huge fish have been caught there in recent years."

One of my Dad's favorite spots from yesteryear that still produces today is the old rock jetties along the south shoreline. The rocks hold lots of baitfish and shrimp—and plenty of hefty specks.

Rue prefers to fish the jetties on a light incoming tide and look for concentrations of mullet to find fish. Mullet are one of the real key elements here, especially when you're looking for trophy trout. The Old Jetties is also a great spot to fish at night. Green lights set up along the rocks draw incredible concentrations of baitfish and equally impressive numbers of trout. Live shrimp is a good bait choice for night fishing, but soft plastics in glow, chartreuse, or white colors can yield strong catches.

GALVESTON/TRINITY BAY

The Galveston Bay complex offers a mind-boggling array of speckled trout habitat by its sheer size alone. One of the hottest and most overlooked spots is the Intracoastal Canal, which intersects several sections of this massive bay. The Anahuac Refuge shoreline is anoth-

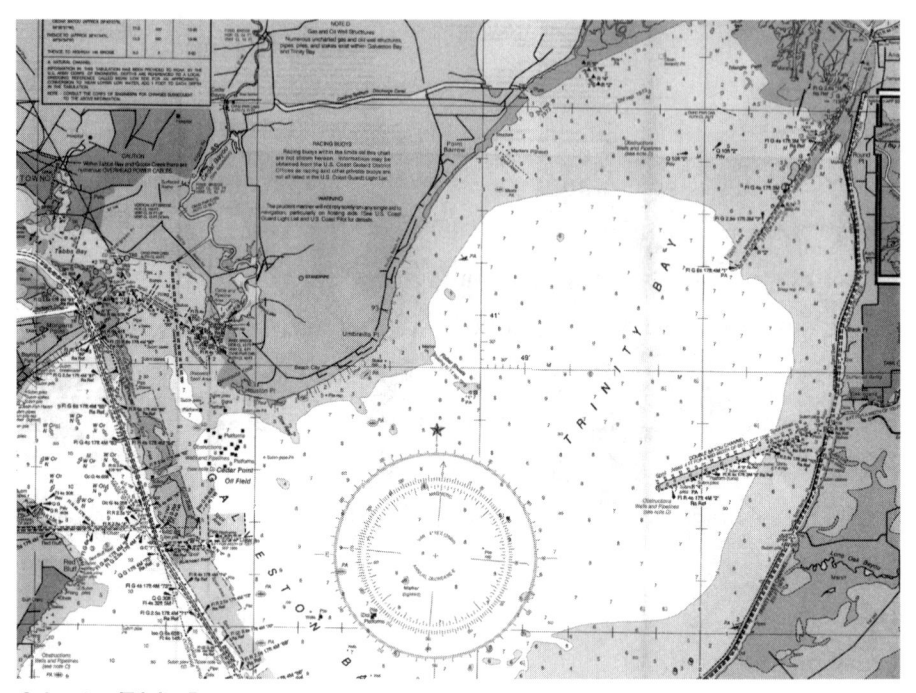

Galveston/Trinity Bays.

er sure bet for trout, along with Smith's Point, Chocolate Bayou, and the south shoreline of East Galveston Bay.

The Texas City flats on Galveston Bay proper is another fruitful fishing location. Ditto for the boat cuts at the north and south jetties. During winter, the Houston Light & Power Canal holds good numbers of trout. In fact, that canal is probably the best place along the coast to find large numbers of trout in winter. The canal is fed by warm power plant water and draws in a huge array of baitfish and the predators that feed on them.

BAFFIN BAY

Baffin Bay means big speckled trout to most fishermen familiar with this isolated destination. That has been true ever since Jim Wallace broke the state record for speckled trout with his 13-pound, 11-

ounce monster sow caught 7 February 1996. Since then, anglers have been looking at Baffin Bay as the premiere place to catch a monster trout.

Practically speaking, most folks know they will never catch such a mammoth fish, but the possibility is enough to keep any self-respecting angler plugging away in this remote spot on the Coastal Bend. Baffin Bay guide Craig West has the perfect story to prove why this is so. Four years ago, he caught a 36-inch fish that weighed just over 13 pounds with a large mullet in its stomach. In comparison, Wallace's record breaker measured only 33 inches. Had West caught that fish before spawning, it would likely have shattered Wallace's record.

If you believe what you hear around bait camps and fishing shows, several 14-pound trout have turned up in the nets of Texas Parks &

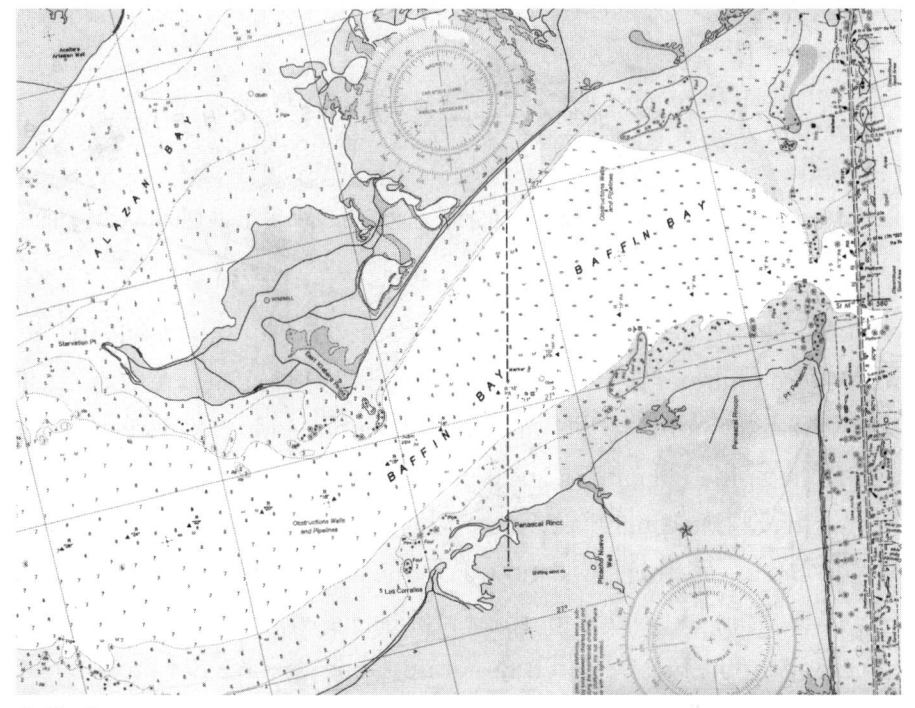

Baffin Bay.

Capt. Mike Denman is all smiles after catching a nice stringer of trout while wading his home body of water.

Wildlife Department (TPWD) survey crews and shrimp trawls in the near-shore Gulf out of Baffin. Of course, TPWD has no knowledge of these fish. According to TPWD Upper Laguna Madre ecosystems biologist Kyle Spiller: "I cannot speak for what the shrimpers have caught, but we have not caught any record-breaking fish in our survey nets. We do catch some big sows and we even caught and tagged a 32-incher, but as far as I know, all of those stories are wives' tales. People like to talk about big fish we catch in our nets, but we have not broken the state record yet."

Spiller said anglers often ask why Baffin Bay has such tremendous trout, but many do not like the answer: "I think a lot of people want a magic answer like 'genetics' or something, but as far as we can tell, there are a lot of factors that go into making an area like Baffin a trophy trout producer. There may, in fact, be some genetic influence, but there's also nutrition, age class, and habitat to consider. Baffin Bay and the Laguna Madre system have an average of about one degree warmer water temperature than Aransas Bay to the north and are even warmer than that in comparison to upper coast bays. That may not seem like much to us, but to a cold-blooded creature, that can mean a lot."

When asked if this could be related to the situation with the huge bass that are produced in the extra warm waters of Florida and California in comparison to the fish caught in Texas, Spiller said that is a good analogy: "We're not sure of all of the factors that go into making Baffin so good for big fish, but that could very well be the point. Also, reputation has something to do with it. This area has got the reputation for producing big fish and the catches to back it up, but there are big trout in many Texas bays besides this one."

Baffin has lots of hotspots including the Gauge Bar and Starvation Point. Both East and West Kleberg points are also excellent, particularly for wade-fishing in late winter and spring

The unusual rock mounds that help define Baffin Bay also harbor some of the better fish, particularly during summer. It is been millions of year since prehistoric worms created the mounds of rocks, but I would be willing to bet lots of anglers would like to go back in time and thank them for doing so. Those rocks are like a magnet to Baffin's big speckled trout.

Capt. Les Cobb of Baffin Bay Guide Service said live croaker fished around these rocks and out into the mouth are a killer method for big sow trout: "During summer, croaker are hard to beat in Baffin. By that time, most of the shrimp in the bay have disappeared, and the trout go to feeding on croaker real heavy. They've produced some huge fish."

If using croakers is not your thing, stick with big topwater to tease those big trout. If the water is murky, go with something in chartreuse or orange. Those colors seem to produce well here.

A note for anglers who have never fished these rocks: It is like fishing any kind of structure. If you do not find fish soon, move on to others. You might have to move to several sets of rocks during the course of a day, but one of them usually pays off.

CHANDELEUR ISLANDS

These barrier islands located off the coasts of Louisiana and Mississippi are widely known for phenomenal speckled trout fishing. Hurricanes Katrin and Rita severely damaged them but the fishing is still good. Anglersroutinely charter trips on houseboats that stay in the islands, acting as a "mother ship" for forays in smaller boats to seek fish.

Lodges at the Chandeleur Islands are a favorite place of vacationers looking for solitude and intense fishing action. This area is one of the author's favorite places to seek speckled trout.

I have fished the islands twice, and absolutely fell in love with the place. Any of the islands can hold trout, but the shallow coves of Breton Island and the surf side of Curlew Island are especially good for wade-fishing. Abundant trout and super-clear water makes fishing highly enjoyable, but beware of stingrays. The Chandeleur Islands may be the stingray capital of the world. I have seen as many as 200 in one small cove.

SABINE LAKE

Sabine Lake is one the most talked about speckled trout fishing destinations on the Gulf Coast. That is because the water body record for speckled trout was broken there twice in 1999, first by Jay Wester of Port Arthur last February with a 10-pound, 3-ounce fish and again a month later by Kelly Rising of Beaumont with an 11-pound, 8-ounce sow caught on the Louisiana shoreline.

As recently as the mid-1990s, if you were running across Sabine Lake and saw somebody wade-fishing, you might think you were dreaming. This area is not exactly known as a wade-fishing hot spot, but that could be changing. Every winter, Capt. Daniel Pyle of Stateline Guide Service catches several trout in the 9-pound category while wading the north end in February and March.: "A lot of people do not realize that the biggest trout of the year can be caught in winter by wade-fishing. The fish do not bite much, but the size is there. On the trips we made, the smallest fish we caught weighed more than 4 pounds. I'll take that kind of 'small fish' any day of the week.

"Now, do not get the idea that we were just mopping on the fish. Among three of us, we might only catch three or four fish apiece, but they're usually very big fish. It is a trade-off. You look for either numbers or size."

Pyle catches these trout while wading shallow, flat areas adjacent to deeper water. The trout like to hold in deep holes during cold weather but move onto the flats to feed on sunny days: "The water temperature rises a few degrees in the shallow areas, and it draws in bait, which in turn draws in the trout. The reason that areas like Laguna Madre are famous for winter trout fishing is that the Intracoastal runs through it and the rest of it is shallow, so you've got vast amounts of good fishing area. Here, you just have to search around and find conducive wading spots."

Pyle said the key to his success is a slow-sinking, soft plastic bait called the Corky. Ever since Jim Wallace broke the state record for speckled trout on a Corky, the bait became extremely popular from the Coastal Bend on down. Now, upper coast anglers are catching on: "For cold water fishing, you just cannot beat it. The Corky is a big-trout specific bait because it sinks very slowly. It is probably the slowest sinking bait on the market. To work the bait, you throw it out and let it sink, and then twitch it a couple of times to give it some action. It drives the fish crazy."

As far as the popularity of wading in this area goes, Lake Sabine guide Capt. Skip James receives a lot of questions from prospective waders: "At just one fishing tradeshow, I got dozens of inquiries about wading Sabine. Seems we're sort of the last frontier for wading. Everybody knows what South Texas has got, now they're wanting to take a look at our fishing."

James does not do much wading himself, but he, too, has started targeting bigger speckled trout: "A lot of my customers are looking for numbers of fish, so I have gone to fishing shad, which is a real killer for trout here, especially in summer and fall. We're catching more big fish on shad fished around areas like East Pass and Coffee Ground Cove than we've ever caught before.

"Croaker is the big thing in Baffin Bay, Galveston, and other

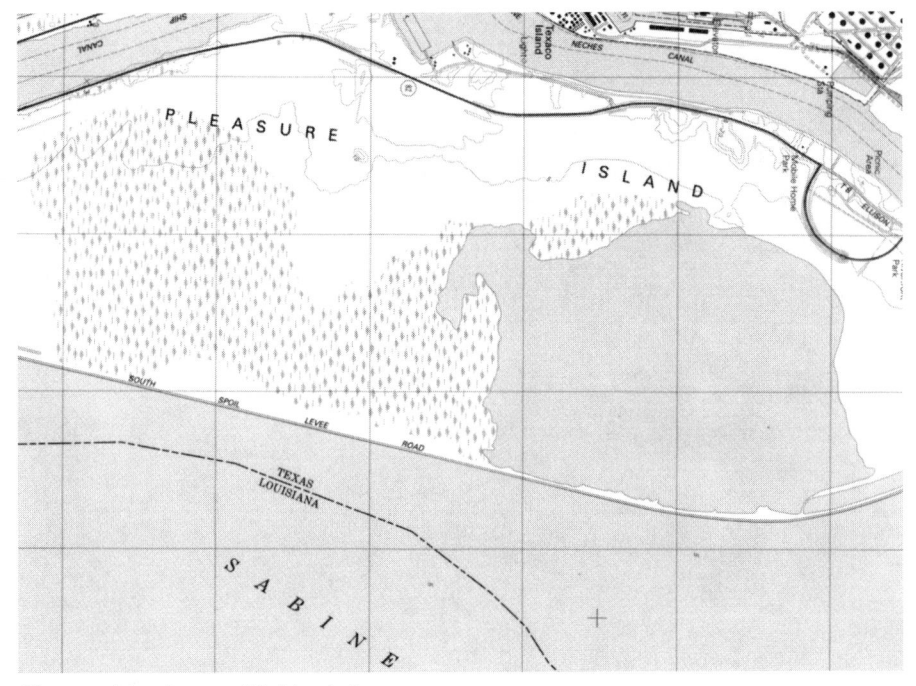

Pleasure Island area of Sabine Lake.

places, but nothing produces like shad over here. I'm an artificial man at heart, but fishing these shad is too effective to ignore, and it is lots of fun. When the lake is too rough, you can anchor in the passes and throw out shad and usually come up with a nice stringer."

Shad fishing took off in 1997 when a shad-caught fish won the annual Orange County Association for Retarded Children benefit tournament. It was the largest trout ever weighed at the August event.

LAGUNA MADRE

South Texas' Laguna Madre is a prime trout fishing destination. The lower sections get plenty of praise, but the upper realms are highly underrated. That is because it is located near Baffin Bay, which many consider the Promised Land of trout fishing. That does not mean Upper

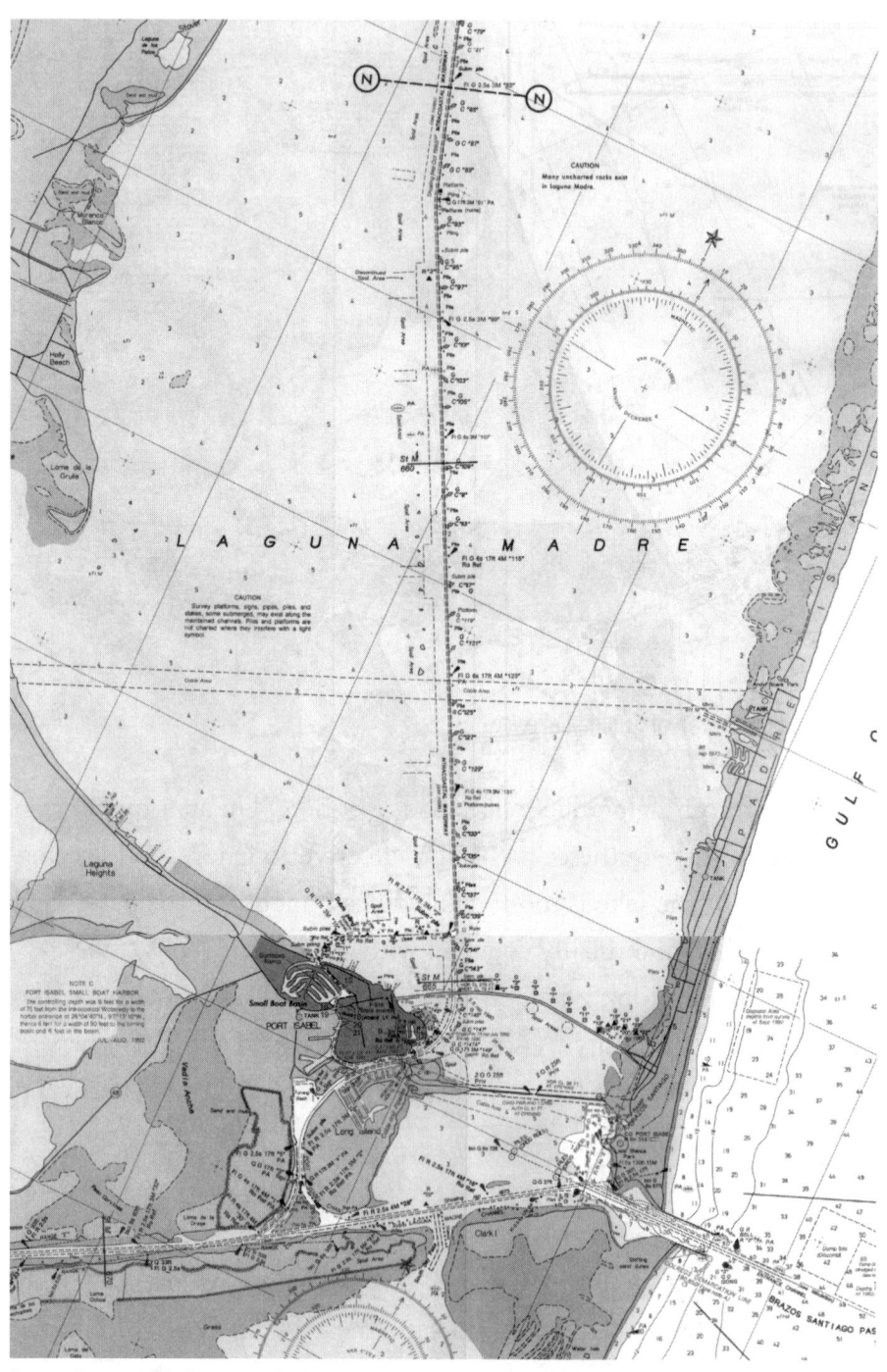

Saltwater Strategies Book Series: **TEXAS TROUT TACTICS**

Lower Laguna Madre

Laguna Madre does not offer up some tremendous fishing opportunities.

Capt. Don Hand gives Upper Laguna Madre a big thumbs up as a potential hangout for hefty trout during late spring and summer: "I would work the area over by putting down the trolling motor and easing down the edge of the channels. This area is especially good when the tide is low and the sides are dry. If the tide is in, expect to see tailing trout on the edge of the grass, even during the heat of the day."

Lure-wise, Hand recommended big topwaters or a Bass Assassin rigged with only a hook for best results: "Lots of guys like fishing the topwaters because they seem to weed out lots of smaller trout, and that is true to an extent. But soft plastic jerkbaits like an Assassin will also catch big fish. I have caught some good ones on it in the past."

Another good method is to drift the shoreline with live shrimp, free-lined or under an Alameda Rattling Float or Mansfield Mauler rig. Hand recommended keying on this area when the water is very clear. This area often turns on in early June when light southeasterly winds push clear water up from Port Mansfield. With clear water comes good fishing.

Any of the shorelines of the islands adjacent to the ship channel can provide a good topwater bite early in the mornings, especially of the wind lays. People get the impression that you cannot fish a topwater when there's wind, but that is not necessarily so. Calm days are usually better for a topwater bite, but a lot of that has to do with locating feeding fish. It is easier to locate feeding fish on calm days.

East Galveston Bay

East Galveston Bay is probably the most consistent producer of big speckled trout on the Texas Coast. Sure, Baffin holds the state record, and the shallow, clear waters of Laguna Madre may be more glamorous, but year in and year out, East Galveston Bay delivers big trout—and lots of them.

Capt. George Knighten looks to the passes to find speckled trout during spring. Baitfish can be scarce in other places this time of year, but the passes offer a constant influx of various forage species: "One of the top spots is Fat Rat Pass. Working a topwater plug like the MirrOlure Top Dog or Top Dog Jr. is a great way to find big fish in that area. Sometimes in early spring, the fishing is not good as far as numbers go, but the quality of the fish is there. If you fish with a big trout-seeking bait like a Top Dog, you up the odds of getting a wall-hanger."

Rollover Bay, located just north of Rollover Pass, is an often-overlooked big trout spot. During the first big tides of spring, a large amount of baitfishes move through the area, so trout often congregate there. Slow-sinking soft plastics, like a Saltwater Assassins or Glass Shad, are good number producers. For big fish, go with topwaters or a Dorky Mullet.

Wade-fishing along the south shoreline of the bay is productive into early summer. Look for concentrations of mullet that attract trout this time of year. The concentrations do not have to be huge. Good numbers of trout can be found under relatively small schools of mullet. I once caught a near-limit in Rollover Bay while fishing around a school of a half-dozen mullet. It was the only bait I could see, so I fished it and hit pay dirt. Sometimes, less is more.

As summer temperatures heat coastal waters, the action shifts to the reefs. Hannah's Reef is a well-known destination for trout enthusiasts. The general practice here is to make long drifts with the current and fish live croaker on the bottom. Specks are suckers for the vocal baitfish, and local marinas regularly sell out quickly when the action is hot and heavy.

Artificial enthusiasts can do well bouncing soft plastics like the Norton Sand Eel and Sabine Snake on the bottom. Hang-ups are inevitable, but that is the name of the game in reef fishing. A drift sock can aid greatly by slowing the drift. If the current is strong, which it often is, a lure cannot be fished properly. Slowing the drift allows a more lifelike presentation and easier bite detection.

During fall, wade-fishing comes back into play. Capt. Rian Glasscock of Complete Sportsman Outfitters said the shorelines turn on again and become the best spots in the entire Galveston Bay system: "During fall, the shoreline over there can be just alive with fish. Specks and reds are actively feeding and are fairly easy to locate, even for anglers who might not be familiar with the area. The key is to not get confused by all of the action and stick with a proven, producing pattern. This usually pays off."

By "proven producing pattern," Glasscock is referring to patterns that have proven successful year in and year out. If you want to catch fish on topwater, stay with them. If you're looking for numbers, go with plastics. "Sometimes, there can be so much action you lose sight of things, but if you stick with your original plan, things will usually work out," he said.

Rollover Pass

Land-bound trout anglers looking to score on speckled trout might want to try Rollover Pass off of Highway 87 in Gilchrist. This area is best known for its fall croaker and flounder runs, but speckled trout are frequently caught in the pass as well.

Tourists typically go about fishing for them by soaking a piece of dead shrimp on the bottom, and, predictably, more often than not their bait is stolen by hardheads, piggy perch, and grunts. Artificial lures would be the best way to work around the bait thieves if it weren't for the fact that spells of good fishing bring in bunches of anglers. Trying to work a lure from the bank while surrounded by anglers with lines

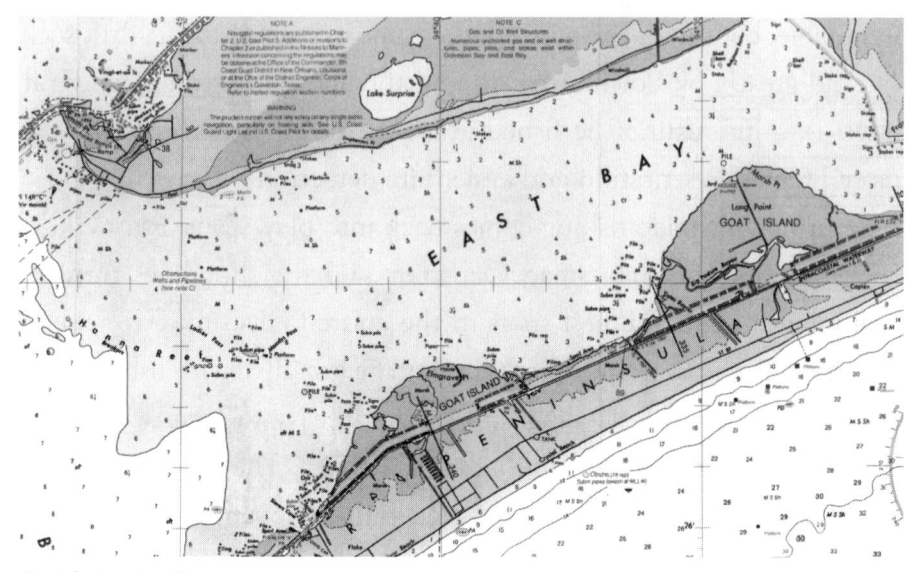

East Galveston Bay

in the water is both difficult and unsafe. It can lead to tangled lines and maybe a bloody nose if you put a hook in someone's kid.

The best bet for fishing here is to use something live. While live shrimp may fall easily to bait stealers, mud minnows, shad, and croaker are more theft-resistant and have longer hook life. Mud minnows are the standard issue in these parts due to the excellent flounder fishing and will more than suffice for trout. Savvy anglers fish with mud minnows under green fishing lights at night. Try it, and you will be surprised at how effective these hardy baitfish really are.

BANK FISHING SPOTS

There are too many good bank-fishing spots on the Gulf Coast to detail all of them, so we will limit our exploration to the better, and a few esoteric ones.

Some overlooked spots in Texas include the Lower Neches Wildlife Management Area off Highway 87 and Lake Road in Bridge City, and various small areas near Matagorda and Palacios. One of these areas is the mouth of Oyster Lake (known as Palacios Bayou) where a bridge crosses the bayou. It is located about 15 miles south of Collegeport, Texas, on Tres Palacios Bay. There's also a small bridge over Turtle Bayou on Highway 35 about one mile west of Palacios that offers some good fishing from time to time.

All of these areas are wheelchair accessible. In the Corpus Christi area, the small rock jetties along the beach on the bay provide some excellent fishing, especially at night with green lights.

In Louisiana and Mississippi, the National Wildlife Refuge system offers excellent bank fishing opportunities. Consult their offices to get maps and details on fishing rules, which can sometimes be tricky on federal land.

chapter twelve

Trout recipes, preparation, & preservation:
From the bay to the table

One of the most rewarding parts about catching speckled trout is eating them. These fish have light, delicate meat that tantalizes the taste buds. It is good stuff.

One of my fondest fishing memories is of my father and me catching a nice stringer of trout on silver spoons in the Bolivar surf, then going back to the beach cabin we rented and frying them. I can still taste those delicious fish 15 years later.

For many years, trout were a popular commercial fish sold in seafood markets from Corpus Christi to Cape Cod. Conservation groups got trout and redfish netting banned and the fishery improved immediately. Netting often killed the biggest and best of the trout population. There is still a commercial trout fishery in the State of Louisiana, but it is limited to rod and reel fishing. The annual take is minute compared to the strike nets that were banned in 1997.

Today, if someone wants to eat speckled trout they have to catch their own. If they want to have a truly tasty meal, they need to handle the trout correctly.

KEEPING TROUT ALIVE

For best results at the dinner table, it's best to keep trout alive as

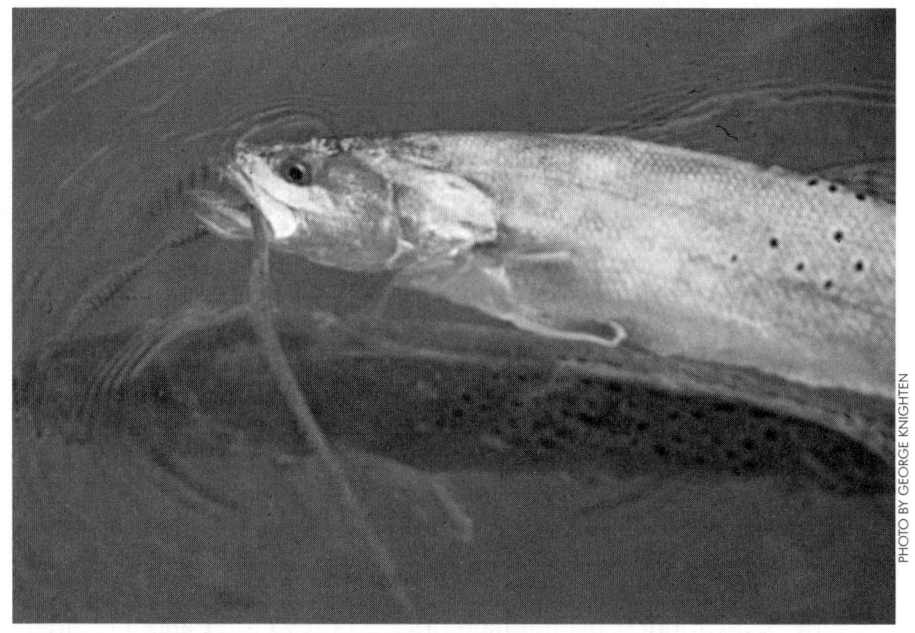

If you use a stringer to keep trout alive, be sure to run it through the lips, not the gills.

long as possible. If you use a stringer to keep fish alive in the field, it's important to insert it correctly. Never run the stringer through the gills. The fish will die quickly. The right way to stringer a trout is to run the stringer through both lips, leaving a little slack so oxygen-carrying water flow into the mouth and through the gills.

When fishing from a boat, I usually just ice them down immediately. This is the preferred method as it ensures the freshest fillets without risking spoilage from premature death. The right way to ice down trout is to lay the fish on a layer of crushed ice, then cover them with another layer. Don't let the fish stay in water, even if it's ice cold. This will soften the meat and hasten spoilage. Keep ice chests well drained.

FREEZING FOR THE FUTURE

Trout meat doesn't freeze as well as red snapper or flounder, but there are ways to ensure tasty trout fillets from the freezer. The following are tips from retail food store chain HEB.

> **METHOD 1:** The recommended method is to wrap fish tightly in plastic wrap or a similar moisture- and vapor-proof material. Keep as much air as possible out of the package. Over-wrap packaged fish with freezer paper or aluminum foil to protect the plastic wrap.
>
> **METHOD 2:** Place fish in zippered plastic freezer bags. Press the bag gently to remove air, or use a straw to suck air out of bag. Seal the bag. Over-wrap packaged fish with freezer paper or aluminum foil to protect the freezer bag.
>
> **METHOD 3:** Place fish in 1-inch thick rigid plastic sandwich containers or milk cartons. Fill container just below the top [with fillets]. Cover the fish with water and seal to prevent drying or oxidation of the fish during storage.
>
> Label packages with type of fish and date. Freeze quickly in single layers in the freezer.

Wrapping fish or immersing in water before freezing helps stave off "freezer burn," or more accurately, "freezer drying." Even frozen water—ice—evaporates over time in a process called "sublimation." This not only removes moisture but also breaks down the meat or other foods at the molecular level, destroying flavor and texture. Another pre-freeze preparation might be the best of all at preventing freezer burn—vacuum-sealed plastic bags. Home vacuum sealing machines and bags are relatively inexpensive and easy to find. These gadgets evacuate virtually all air from a tough, boilable, freezable plastic bag, then heat-seal it 100 percent airtight. Wal-Mart carries the Food Saver Vac 500 model. I have also seen them hawked on TV infomercials.

Freezing Smoked Fish

Freeze smoked fish as soon as you remove it from the smoker. Brush pieces of smoked fish with bland salad oil, if you desire, to slow dehydration and oxidation during frozen storage. Choose one of the packaging methods described above for freezing smoked fish.

Thawing Frozen Seafood

Thaw frozen seafood in the refrigerator (about 18 hours for a 1-inch thick package) or under cold running water (about one hour for a 1-inch thick package). Do not thaw frozen seafood at room temperature or under warm running water. Thinner parts of the seafood thaw faster than thicker parts, and the outer edges may start to spoil or dry out before the center has thawed.

RECIPES

BARBECUED SPECKLED TROUT

1 small trout, whole
Flour
Corn oil
Salt & pepper; to taste
Tabasco

Wash the fish and dry with a paper towel. Make a paste from the flour and corn oil, seasoned with salt, pepper, and Tabasco. Coat the fish with the thin paste. Place over a medium-heat grill about three inches from the charcoal briquettes. Barbecue 6 to 8-minutes, turning the fish once. Allow one fish per person. Any white fish will work

BAKED TROUT WITH SEAFOOD

4 trout, 16 oz each, cleaned
1/2 lb. butter or margarine
2 Tbs. flour
1-1/2 cup dry white wine
2 Tbs. lime juice
3/4 cup light cream
18 oysters
3/4 lb. Peeled shrimp

Blend melted butter or margarine and flour. Add white wine and lime juice and heat. Place trout into baking dish or pan. Sprinkle with salt and pepper; pour sauce over fish. Cover and bake 10-15 minutes at 375 degrees, basting 2 to 3 times. Add light cream, oysters, and peeled shrimp. Bake covered 20 minutes or until shrimp are done.

HERBED TROUT WITH SOUR CREAM

4 6-oz. trout fillets
1 Tbs. chopped parsley
1/4 cup dry white wine
2 Tbs. Butter
1/3 cup sour cream
1 Tbs. chopped onion
1 pinch chervil
1/4 cup soft bread crumbs; buttered
1 pinch tarragon
salt and pepper

Rinse fillets, pat dry with paper towels, and sprinkle lightly with salt and pepper. Grease four pieces of heavy aluminum foil. Place a trout fillet on each. Melt butter and sauté onion 2 minutes. Add wine, parsley, chervil, and tarragon. Divide mixture evenly over each trout. Wrap tightly and place packages on a raised rack in a greased baking pan. Bake at 450 for 15 minutes or until fish flakes easily with a fork. Carefully open packages and gently remove the fillets and topping, allowing the liquid to drain away. Remove the racks, discard any liquid remaining in the baking pan, and return fillets to the pan. Spread 1/4 of sour cream over each trout fillet and sprinkle with bread crumbs. Broil until lightly browned.

KENNET FRIED TROUT

2 small trout (6-8 oz each)
2 pieces thick cut bacon
1 Tbs. (heaped) coarse oatmeal
2 oz. unsalted or clarified butter
1 lemon, juiced
plain flour

Rub the skins of the cleaned and dried trout very gently with a good grinding of pepper. Dust lightly with flour and salt. Warm a frying pan large enough to take the two fish and toast the oatmeal in it. Remove and reserve. Cut the bacon into snippets and fry gently until the fat runs, then increase heat to crisp the bacon a little. Remove and keep hot. Dice the butter and add 1-1/2 oz. to pan. When the butter foam dies down, add the fish, pressing them down lightly so they lie very flat. After 4-5 minutes steady cooking in the bubbling butter, the skin on the underside of the fish should be crisp and golden brown. Turn carefully and fry on the other side in the same way. Put the cooked fish on warmed plates, scatter the bacon and oatmeal over them, and keep hot. Wipe out the pan with a paper towel. Melt the remaining butter and cook to a rich shade of gold. Add lemon juice and a little salt and pepper. Swirl to mix well, pour over the trout, and serve immediately with lemon wedges.

SESAME FRIED TROUT

1 egg
1 Tbs. Water
4 Tbs. sesame seed
1 cup bread crumbs
1/4 cup flour
4 Trout (about 3 lbs.)
1/4 cup vegetable oil

Beat egg with water. Mix sesame seeds and bread crumbs. Coat fish with flour. Dip fish in egg mixture and roll in sesame seeds and breadcrumbs. Pan fry in hot oil about 10 minutes per side or until flesh flakes from bones.

TROUT AND SOUR CREAM

1 fish per person
1 oz unsalted butter per fish
2 Tbs. sour cream
2 Tbs. water per fish
salt and pepper

The fish should be very fresh, gutted, and scaled, but not split. Melt the butter. When it foams, slip in the fish. Brown swiftly, turning once. Pour the sour cream and water around them, add salt and freshly ground pepper, and simmer for 10 minutes.

SOURDOUGH STUFFED TROUT

1 small loaf sourdough or crusty Italian bread
2 Tbs. finely chopped parsley
1/2 tsp. salt
1/8 tsp. pepper
1/2 cup thinly sliced green onions (include tops)
1 medium bell pepper, finely chopped
3 Tbs. dry white wine
1/4 cup melted butter or margarine
6 whole cleaned trout (approx. 15 inches long)
salt and pepper

Preheat oven to 400. Cut enough bread into 1/2-inch cubes to make 2 cups (reserve remainder for other uses). Spread bread cubes in single layer on baking sheet and bake, stirring occasionally, until cubes are dry and crisp (about 10 minutes). Remove from oven and pour into a bowl. Combine with parsley, salt, pepper, green onion, and bell pepper. Drizzle wine and 2 Tbs. of the butter over bread and mix lightly.

Wipe fish with damp cloth, inside and out. Brush cavities with some of the remaining butter; sprinkle lightly with salt and pepper. Stuff cavities loosely with bread mixture, dividing mixture evenly among fish. Skewer edges together or sew with heavy cotton thread (nylon can burn and impart unpleasant flavor). Arrange fish side by side in a greased shallow baking pan (use 2 pans, if necessary). Drizzle any remaining butter evenly over tops of fish. Bake fish, uncovered, until it flakes readily when prodded in thickest portion with a fork.

TROUT ITALIAN

4 8-oz. trout fillets
Italian salad dressing

Place the trout fillets in a shallow bowl and cover with Italian salad dressing. Marinate for about 2 hours. Place trout on a well oiled grill about 5 inches from the heat. Cook for 5 minutes or until fish flakes easily when tested with a fork. Garnish with fresh parsley.

TROUT WITH HORSERADISH SAUCE

2 6-oz. trout fillets
dry vermouth or white wine
1 Tbs. dill, minced
1/2 cup sour cream
2 small cucumbers, sliced
1 white horseradish, minced and drained

Bring to a rolling boil enough vermouth or wine to half fill a small pan. Place a rack over pan. Steam fillets on rack for 9 to 10 minutes. Remove from rack and cool. Combine sour cream, horseradish, and dill weed for dressing. Trout may be served cold with sour cream dressing. Garnish with cucumber slices. Serves 2.

CRABBY STUFFED TROUT

1/4 cup minced celery
1/2 cup minced onion
1/2 cup minced fresh parsley
1/2 cup minced shallots
1 clove minced garlic
1/2 cup melted butter
1 Tbs. all-purpose flour
1/2 cup milk
1/2 cup dry white wine
1/2 lb. crab meat
1-1/4 cups seasoned dry bread crumbs
1/4 tsp. salt
1/4 tsp. pepper
6 8-oz trout fillets, halved crosswise
paprika

In a large skillet, sauté, celery, onion, parsley, shallots, green pepper, and garlic in butter over medium heat until vegetables are tender. Add flour, and cook 1 minute, stirring constantly. Gradually add milk and wine, stirring constantly until mixture is slightly thickened. Remove from heat and stir in crab meat, breadcrumbs, salt, and pepper. Place 6 fillet halves in a greased jelly roll pan. Spoon about 1/2 cup crab meat stuffing onto each fillet. Cut remaining fillet halves in half lengthwise. Place a fillet quarter on each side of stuffed fillets in jelly roll pan, pressing gently into stuffing mixture. Sprinkle with paprika. Bake at 425 for 15 to 20 minutes or until fish flakes easily when tested with a fork.

BOILED SPECKLED TROUT

4 speckled trout
fresh onion tops
fresh thyme
fresh bay leaf
10 cloves
24 fresh allspice, mashed fine
small piece lemon peel
1 red pepper

Clean and wash fish thoroughly, score with an "S" on back. Lace twine around the body of the fish to keep it together (never tie in a cloth). To boiling water, add onion tops, thyme, bay leaf, cloves, allspice, lemon peel, and red pepper. Boil about 10 minutes, then slip fish in carefully to avoid breaking. Boil another 10 minutes and remove from water. Drain, lay on a platter, sprinkle thickly with minced parsley, and serve with butter sauce. Serves 4.

THYME TROUT

1-1/2 lbs. trout fillets
8 tsp. mayonnaise
1/2 tsp. dried thyme
1/8 tsp. grated lemon peel
2 Tbs. dry breadcrumbs
salt and pepper

Preheat oven to 350. Place fish in a lightly oiled shallow baking pan. Combine all ingredients except breadcrumbs in a bowl, salt and pepper to taste. Spread mixture evenly over fillets. Sprinkle with breadcrumbs. Bake uncovered 30 minutes or until fish flakes easily. Serve with wild rice.

Trout Spaghetti

2 lbs. fresh trout filets
16 oz. cream cheese
1/2 cup milk
2 Tbs. butter
1 Tbs. olive oil
1 clove garlic, minced
1 small onion, diced
1 Tbs. rosemary
1 Tbs. basil
1 Tbs. oregano
salt & pepper
pasta cooked *al dente*

Cut fillets into 1/2-inch cubes. Melt butter in olive oil over medium-high heat until bubbling. Toss cubed trout and sear, turning or tossing to cook all sides. Remove from skillet and set aside. Combine milk, cream cheese, minced garlic, diced onion, rosemary, basil, and oregano into a smooth sauce. Add to skillet and combine with remaining oil and butter, simmer 15 to 20 minutes. Add cubed trout filets and simmer another 10 minutes. Serve over pasta. Serves 6-8.

Trout Amandine with Creole Sauce

6 8-ounce trout fillets, skinned
Creole seasoning
1 cup milk
2 cups flour
2 Tbs. butter
1/3 cup olive oil
3/4 cup Worcestershire sauce
2 lemons, peel and pith removed
2 bay leaves
3/4 pound cold butter, cubed

1 cup sliced almonds
1 Tbs. chopped parsley
2 Tbs. chopped green onions

Sprinkle seasonings on fillets, place in a glass bowl, and cover with milk. Cover and refrigerate 1 hour. Drain fillets. Add Creole seasoning to flour and dredge fillets, covering completely. In a large skillet, heat 2 Tbs. butter in olive oil. Fry fillets 3 to 4 minutes per side until golden brown. Season drained fillets again with more seasonings or salt and pepper to taste, and set aside.

Drain oil from skillet, leaving the browned bits in the bottom. Stir in Worcestershire sauce, lemons, and bay leaves. Simmer until reduced by 2/3. Whisk in cold butter cubes one at a time. (The sauce should be thick and coat the back of a spoon.) Stir in almond slices. Spoon sauce over fish and garnish with parsley and green onions. Serves 6.

BEER BATTER FISH FRY

1 cup all-purpose flour
1 egg, beaten
1 tsp. garlic powder
1/2 tsp. black pepper
1 to 1-1/2 cups beer

In a small mixing bowl, combine flour, egg, garlic powder, and black pepper. Stir in 1 cup beer (you can add more to obtain desired texture). Coat fish with batter and fry as normal. Use on any white fish.

TROUT WITH BANANAS

2 Tbs. butter
1 Tbs. all-purpose flour
1 cup milk
6 trout fillets
1/2 cup white wine
2 Tbs. fresh lime juice
3 bananas, sliced lengthwise
1/4 cup grated Parmesan cheese
salt and pepper to taste

Preheat oven to 350. In a medium saucepan over medium heat, blend the butter, flour, and milk. Cook, stirring constantly, until thick sauce forms. Arrange trout in a single layer in a medium baking dish and cover with the wine and lime juice. Season with salt and pepper. Pour half the sauce over the fish. Arrange bananas over the fish and cover with remaining sauce. Sprinkle with Parmesan cheese. Bake 25 minutes until cheese is lightly browned and fish flakes easily. Drain remaining juices before serving.

BAKED TROUT IN GARLIC AND OLIVE OIL

4 trout fillets
4 cloves garlic, crushed
3 Tbs. olive oil
1 onion, chopped
1/4 tsp. cayenne pepper

Rub fillets with garlic and place them in a shallow glass or plastic dish. Sprinkle with onion. Cover and refrigerate overnight. Transfer to 9x13 baking dish and drizzle with olive oil. Sprinkle with cayenne or white pepper. Bake in preheated 350 oven for 30 minutes.

You can also grill by wrapping fish and seasonings in foil.

chapter thirteen

Making Book:
Putting one in the record books

Landing a record-sized speckled trout is something most coastal fishermen fantasize about. Who would not want to battle a mammoth sow speck bigger than any other caught by an angler? Of course, this is mostly a pipe dream on the world record level, but there are plenty of opportunities for water body, line class, and, to a lesser degree, state records for trout.

First, let's look at the requirements of the angler recognition and records programs sponsored by the Texas Parks & Wildlife Department. The following are rules for all state and water body records:

>State record applications must be notarized.
>**For length measurement:**
>Place fish on its side with the jaw closed.
>Squeeze the tail fin together or turn it in a way to obtain the maximum overall length.
>Measure a straight line from the tip of the snout to the

extreme tip of the tail fin.

Fish must be weighed on certified scales within three days of the catch date. Certified scales are scales (either electronic or spring-based) that have been certified as accurate by the Texas Department of Agriculture or a commercial scales calibration company. A partial list of certified scales is available online.

One or more witnesses must observe the weighing.

One witness must be the owner or employee of the business maintaining the certified scale.

The weighmaster may not be the angler.

The fish must not contain anything or have anything attached which artificially increases weight.

Photographs must be submitted with application.

Species verification is required. TPWD fisheries biologists will identify the species from the photographs submitted with the application. If biologists are unable to make a conclusive identification from the photographs, then the angler must provide the fish (whole and intact except for grass carp and tilapia which must have the intestines removed immediately) for physical/scientific examination. If the angler is unable to provide the fish for examination, the record claim will not be considered.

Here are the rules for fly fishing records.

The lure must be a recognized type of artificial fly.

A fly may be dressed on a single or double hook or two single hooks in tandem. Treble hooks are prohibited. The use of any other type of lure or natural or preserved bait, either singularly or attached to the fly, is prohibited.

No scent, either natural or artificial, is allowed on flies.

The use of scented material in a fly is prohibited.

The rod, reel, line, and leader equipment used must be designed for fly-fishing.

Casting and retrieving must be carried out in accordance with normal customs and generally accepted practices. The major criterion in casting is that the weight of the line must carry the lure rather than the weight of the lure carrying the line.

Here are rules that apply to all reward programs.

The fish must be caught in Texas waters.

An Angler Recognition Award application form (PWD-349H-T3200) completed by the angler must be received by TPWD within 60 days of the date of catch.

The catch must not be at variance with any laws or regulations governing the fish species or the waters in which it was caught. It is unlawful to hunt or fish without a valid license, or a permit and stamp on your person and available for inspection by a game warden, unless exempt by age. Review the TPWD Outdoor Annual regulations booklet or check the Fishing Regulations pages for statewide size, bag and possession limits before going fishing.

Only one person may catch the fish (except for netting or gaffing the fish to bring it into the boat or onto shore).

The fish must not have contained anything (including electronics or other tagging devices) to assist in locating the fish.

Any deliberate falsification of any application will result in disqualification. All existing records will be removed and future applications from the angler will not be considered.

TPWD officials reserve the right to review, investigate, reject, disqualify, or accept any application submitted or any award granted. In case of disputes, the decision of the Angler Recognition Awards Program Committee will be final.

For more information, contact:
Angler Recognition Awards Program
Texas Parks & Wildlife Department
4200 Smith School Road, Austin TX 78744
Email: joedy.gray@tpwd.state.tx.us
Telephone: 512-389-8037

LINE CLASS RECORDS

Line class records are kept by the International Game Fish Association (IGFA), an organization known for its strict guidelines and unparalleled fish record gauging system. A line class record means you have caught the largest specimen of a particular species on a particular pound-test line. For example, there are records for speckled trout on 10-pound-test, 15-pound-test, and 5-pound-test lines, to name but a few. The 5-pound-test line class record fish may weigh 10 pounds, whereas the 15-pound-test record fish may weigh only 8 pounds. It is all matter of the heaviest fish caught on a given line class.

IGFA rules are quite lengthy and would require a separate chapter. It is best to contact them directly:

International Game Fish Association
300 Gulf Stream Way
Dania Beach, FL 33004
Pho. 954-927-2628
Email: igfahq@aol.com

FOR INFORMATION ON STATE RECORDS AND FISHING REGULATIONS ALONG THE GULF COAST CONTACT:

Texas Parks & Wildlife Department
4200 Smith School Road
Austin, TX 78744
512-389-4800

Louisiana Department of Wildlife and Fisheries
P.O. Box 98000
Baton Rouge, LA 70898-9000
504-765-2800

Mississippi Department of Wildlife, Fisheries, and Parks
P.O. Box 451
Jackson, MS 39205
601-362-9212

Alabama Department of Conservation and Natural Resources
64 N. Union St.
Montgomery, AL 36130-1456
334-242-3465

Florida Fish and Wildlife Conservation Commission
620 S. Meridian Street
Tallahassee, FL 32399-1600
904-488-3831

STATE RECORDS FOR SPECKED TROUT

Texas: 15.60 pounds.

Louisiana: 12.38 pounds

Mississippi: 10.6 pounds

Alabama: 12.4 pounds

Florida: 17.7 pounds (also standing world record)

TROUT INFORMATION RESOURCES ON THE WEB

http://www.tpwd.state.tx.us
(Type "speckled trout" in the search engine to find more information than you really wanted to know about the species.)

http://www.speckledtroutclinic.com
(This is a great site with lots of interesting information and theories on trophy trout fishing.)

http://marinefisheries.org/FishID/drumspot.html
(This site has all kinds of good technical information about the species.)

http://tampa.about.com/library/fish/blspottrout.htm
(Let the fish gurus in Florida enlighten you on all matters trout.)

http://dnr.cbi.tamucc.edu/wiki/Main/HomePage
(Get all of your coastal bay conditions here.)

http://www.offshoreweather.com
(Before you fish the short rigs, check this site out. It also has tides from all over the place.)

http://www.gulffishing.com
(Check out great fishing articles as well as tide charts.)

http://www.fishgame.com
(Check out great articles and share fishing tips on this message board.)

http://www.gslis.utexas.edu
(Just plain, good fishing information.)

Chapter 13 | Making book

Jim Wallace, current Texas State speckled trout holder.

207

Saltwater Strategies Book Series: **TEXAS TROUT TACTICS**

Some say the age of the "super trout" is upon us.

chapter fourteen

Super Trout:

Will selective breeding and genetic experiments create super-sized specks?

The future of the spotted seatrout seems bright along the Gulf Coast. With the prohibition of commercial harvest, speckled trout populations have flourished despite increased recreational fishing pressure.

I believe we are about to enter the age of the "super trout." This is not a creature that leaps tall buildings in a single bound, but it could be equally impressive to those who consider *Cynoscion nebulosis* to be tops among saltwater game fish.

In the chapter on short rigs, I recount an encounter with a monstrous speckled trout at an oil platform. Since that encounter, each question seemed to spawn another and another until I found myself at home that night watching a show on the Discovery Channel. It was about bioengineering and the scientists in Europe who are trying to create a "super sheep," an animal that would grow much larger than the average sheep and yield twice the wool. I found myself thinking: *If they can create a "super sheep," why not a "super trout"?* After all, the introduction of Florida bass genes has practically doubled the size of

Saltwater Strategies Book Series: **TEXAS TROUT TACTICS**

Tagging studies, radio telemetry, and genetic altering have helped to increase understanding of speckled trout and may in the future allow scientists to create a bigger, more aggressive fish.

bass in reservoirs throughout Texas and California. Why couldn't scientists isolate the growth genes in speckled trout and create a supreme subspecies to release into our bay systems?

Visions of the monster trout I saw stayed with me as I began a quest to learn more about the possibilities for the creation of a super trout. I discovered that what may seem like science fiction now could be reality in the future.

How close are we?

The first step of my quest was to define exactly what a super trout would be. Make no mistake, a super trout would have to be a gargantuan fish. I'm talking about a fish that would command serious respect in any bay system, making schools of foot-long mullet really nervous. TPWD labels bass weighing 13 pounds or more as "lunkers," so I think a speckled trout weighing more than 10 pounds would qualify as a genuine "super trout."

TPWD fisheries managers are making great strides in genetic coding of speckled trout populations. Researchers at the University of Texas Marine Science Center at Port Aransas have learned how to stimulate growth hormones in the ovaries of trout. A team of Louisiana State University scientists has developed methods for preserving trout sperm so they can perfect trophy-targeted artificial insemination of the species.

Perhaps what's most promising is research by the Marine Gene Probe Laboratory in Maryland. They've created pedigrees for certain species of salmonids. Aquaculturists are paying top dollar for salmonid broodstock that grow extra large, and scientists say it won't be long before they can develop pedigrees for saltwater species like speckled trout.

Don't get the idea that genetics are the answer to everything. TPWD coastal fisheries biologists are quick to point out that good genes may be important for producing big speckled trout, but other factors, including age, nutrition, and environment, also play a role.

TPWD is getting in on big trout mania. They've created the "Texas Gulf Coast Roundup," a program modeled after the ShareLunker program for bass, in which coastal anglers donate live fish for coastal fisheries' projects. They're not seeking speckled trout exclusively, but obtaining top broodstock from different ecosystems is one of their stated goals. They're also talking about "tweaking" speckled trout regulations to produce more trophy fish. Are they trying to create a super trout?

These agencies may not consciously be working toward the creation of the super trout, but you can bet they see the potential of such an accomplishment. The speckled trout is quickly becoming to the saltwater community what the largemouth bass is to freshwater fishermen, and this is creating a serious economic incentive to create bigger, better fish.

Do you think Texas bass fishing would be as popular as it is without the introduction of the Florida bass? TPWD is openly trying to produce a world record bass in Texas. If this happens, it could mean a lot to the sport fishing industry of the Lone Star State. Along the same lines, creating more large trout would seemingly benefit everyone. The key word is "seemingly."

WOULD IT STILL BE A TROPHY?

My initial journey into studying "super trout possibilities" excited me. Who wouldn't want the opportunity to catch a 10-, 12-, or 13-pound trout? The answer to that question gets complicated when considering what a true "trophy" is. I'm a whitetailed deer hunter and

Chapter 14 | Super Trout

When all trout become trophies, will the term "trophy" lose its meaning?

213

would love nothing more than to shoot a Boone & Crockett class buck. Most deer hunters have dreamed of it. But I realize it would be far more exciting to shoot one on open range on my $300-a-year East Texas hunting club than to hit the lotto and shoot a pedigreed, steroid-fed, monster buck that was bought and paid for by a rancher. There would be no real physical differences between the two animals, but the difference in the spiritual qualities of the hunts would be gargantuan. One harvest would be the result of hard hunting and a chance encounter with a truly wild creature. The other would be the result of paying enough cash to get what I wanted.

Much of an animal's beauty is in its wildness. It's one thing to catch a 10-pound largemouth bass in a pond stocked with monsters. It's something else to catch one in the river where 5-pounders—much less double-digit fish—are few and far between.

As *Louisiana Sportsman* Editor Todd Masson noted in a column denouncing Texas' push toward a "trophy" trout fishery, a 10-pound fish will no longer be a trophy if everyone is catching 10-pounders.

While my initial investigation into "super trout" excited me, my latest endeavors have me a bit concerned. I am concerned we are going to make trout fishing synthetic and take the true spirit of the sport away. TPWD is already producing largemouth bass that bite more aggressively than native, wild fish. Will they do this with trout in the future? How far will they and other fish and game departments go? More importantly, how far will we let them go?

BACK AT THE RIG

In April 2002, I returned to the rig for my first short rig fishing of the year. I've been there numerous times since that first encounter with the monster trout, but this time I was in a philosophical mood. I realized that, statistically speaking, I would probably never see such a

Chapter 14 | Super Trout

trout again, neither on my line nor under the water. Of course, I never thought I would find myself face-to-fin with the trout of a lifetime in the first place, so you never know what hand fate is going to deal. When science gets involved, the line between fate and progress often gets blurred. Throw in some economic incentive for good measure, and the chances of seeing the creation of a super trout in the near future could be better than you or I imagine. I'm certainly not against producing bigger and better fish, I just hope the spirit of fishing doesn't get trampled in the process.

The age of the super trout may not yet be here, but it's probably just around the corner.

And an interesting age it should be.

Acknowledgments

Writing the acknowledgements for my books has always been the most challenging part. There are so many people to thank and I certainly do not want to leave anyone out.

I should definitely start with my wife Lisa who I would be lost without and who supports everything I do. I love you very much and look forward to many more years of enjoying this life together.

My daughter Faith has been a new source of inspiration and joy in our lives and makes me want to be a better man every single day.

My parents, Chester and Gloria Moore have supported me from day one and I know they will be there at every turn. Thank you both for being who you are.

To my cousin and partner in crime Frank Moore who I am so proud of for reinventing himself and who usually out fishes me at every turn. You have an amazing family. I love you Jaclyn, Shelton, Lucas and Madison.

This book would not have been possible without the belief and support of Roy and Ardia Neves who somehow saw something in a longhaired, intense wild man from Southeast Texas years ago. Thank you for being such a pleasure to work for and for allowing me to unleash my vision for the outdoors through Texas Fish & Game and this book.

Don Zaidle may look like a grizzly (or maybe a yeti) but he has a sharp mind for editing and he shares my passion for all things wild. Here's to many more conversations about the outdoors, politics and everything in between.

Duane Hruzek has done a great job of promoting the Texas Fish & Game library of books and deserves major kudos for putting out this second edition of Texas Trout Tactics.

Everyone at Texas Fish & Game deserve thanks for being cool people and helping put out a great product: Denise Chavez, Lindsay Whitman, Jimmy Borne, Nicole McKibbin, Denise Bell and the rest of the extended TF&G family.

There are so many people in this business who deserve credit for helping me over the years. I know I will miss a few but here goes: Mark Davis, Bruce Shuler, Garret Scherer, Robert Scherer, the late Ed Holder, Ed Kestler, Jim Love, Al Caldwell, Jaime Landis, Lou Marullo, Ted Nugent, Skip James, Phillip Samuels, Chris Parr, Ted Price, Chris Moody, Steve Roth, Buddy Oakes, Brian Fischer, Shane Chesson, Will Beaty, Tim Soderquist, David Schuessler, Keith Warren, TJ Greany and many others.

I would like to thank the staff at Sea Center Texas for supporting speckled trout conservation. So a big thank you goes to David Abrego, Shane Bonnot, Courtney Moore and everyone who helps make our stocking program happen. You guys are amazing.

I would like to thank my pastors David Berkheimer and Daniel Rose for making Community Church in Orange a great place to worship and for their spiritual leadership.

As always my inspiration come from many places and they often have nothing to do with the outdoors. This time it was Marvel Comics. So thanks to Stan Lee, Jack Kirby and Steve Ditko for creating such amazing characters like the Hulk, Spiderman, Iron Man, the X-Men, The Avengers and so many others. And yes, I am still a big kid. Hulk Smash!

And last but certainly not least thanks to the Lord Jesus Christ for always being there and helping transform my life in a very profound way over the last six years. I am in constant awe.

Index

A

Abu Garcia, 137
    Ambassadeur 5000, 137
Academy Sports & Outdoors, 65
Alabama Department of Conservation and
    Natural Resources, 205
Alameda Rattling Float, 181
Alaska, 126
All Star Rods, 132, 137
    popping rods, 132
Anahuac Wildlife Refuge, 171
Angler Recognition Award Program, 203,
    204
aquaculturists, 211
Aransas Bay, 175
Army Corps of Engineers, 163
artificial lures, 179, 183
Austin, Texas, 205

B

backlash, 69
Baffin Bay, 111, 172, 175, 178, 181
    East and West Kleberg points, 175
    Gauge Bar, 175
    Starvation Point, 175
Baffin Bay Guide Service, 175
baitfish, 165, 171, 182, 184
bank fishing, 155, 183, 184
barracuda, 129
Bass Assassins, 63, 149, 181
Bass fishermen, 146
Baton Rouge, Louisiana, 205
Bayou Charter Service, 169
beach, 155-168, 187
Beaumont, Texas, 147, 177
Berkley, 70
    Big Game monofilament line, 70
    Fireline super line, 66, 137
    Power Mullet, 146
"Bill Dancing", 69
boats, 188
    fiberglass bass, 127
Bolivar Peninsula, 145, 165, 187
Bono, Steve, 169
Boone & Crockett, 214
Bridge City, Texas, 184
brown trout, 124
Burleigh, Gerald, 28

C

California, 175, 211
Cameron jetties, 131, 135, 139, 145, 153
Cameron, Louisiana, 154, 160
cane poles, 121
Cape Cod, 187
catch-and-release, 73
Central Texas, 121
certified scales, 202
Chandeleur Islands, Louisiana, 68, 145, 154, 176
    Breton Island, 177
    Curlew Island, 177
Charlie Slab, 133, 147
Charlie's worm, 163
Chocolate Bayou, 172
Chug Bugs
    Rattlin' Chug Bug, 136, 161
Cobb, Capt. Les, 175
Collegeport, Texas, 185
Complete Sportsman Outfitters, 183
conservation, 187
Constance Beach, Louisiana, 158
Corky, 178
Corpus Christi, Texas, 185, 187
crabs, 153
crankbaits, 65
croaker, 111, 134, 148, 166, 178, 182
    live, 163, 175
"croaker soakers", 114
Culprit
    Rip Tide shrimp tails, 132, 146
    Shrimp tails, 143
Cynoscion nebulosis, 1, 209

D

Daiichi, 74
    Tru-Turn, 74, 148
Daleo, Mike, 153
Dania Beach, Florida, 204
Denman, Capt. Mike, 18, 174

Dillman, Capt. David, 135
Discovery Channel, 209
DOA Lures
    DOA Bait Buster, 160, 161
    DOA Shrimp, 132, 135, 146
Dorky Mullet, 182
Dyson, Dean, 149

E

East Coast, Atlantic, 126
East Galveston Bay, 172, 181
    Fat Rat Pass, 182
    Hannah's Reef, 182
    Rollover Bay, 182
East Texas, 214
Europe, 209
Excalibur fishing lines, 148

F

Florida, 125, 141, 148, 175, 206, 209
Florida Fish and Wildlife Conservation Commission, 205
flounder, 166, 183, 189
Flounder Fundamentals, 67
fly-fishermen, 69
Fly-fishing, 121, 123, 202
free-line, 134
Freeport, Texas, 131
freezer burn, 189
freezer drying, 189
freezing smoked fish, 190

G

Galveston Bay complex, 171, 178, 183
Galveston jetties, 131, 132, 139, 146
Gas wells, 143
Glass Shad, 182
Glasscock, Capt. Rian, 183
GPS (Global Positioning Satellite), 157
green fishing lights, 140, 167, 171, 184
Grumman aluminum boats, 150

Index

grunts, 183
Guadalupe River, 121
Gulf Coast, †4, 123, 131, 158, 163, 170, 177, 209
Gulf Coast Tackle, 147
Gulf of Mexico, 70, 131, 135, 138, 139, 140, 143, 144, 159, 165, 166

H

Hackberry Rod & Gun Club, 69, 170
Hand, Capt. Don, 181
hardhead, 183
Harris, Terry, 165
Hebert, Capt. Malcolm, 140, 141
Hoginar, 147
Houston Light & Power Canal, 172
Houston, Texas, x

I

International Game Fish Association (IGFA), 204

J

jack crevalle, 142
Jackson, Mississippi, 205
James, Capt. Skip, 178
jerkbaits, 149, 181
jetties, 63, 131, 132, 134, 137, 142, 145, 158
    anchors, 140
    currents, 133, 138
    jetty wall, 133
    navigating at night, 140
    rip currents, 138
    safety, 138
"jetty sheepshead rig", 138
jighead, 133
Johnson, Capt. Everett, 126

K

"kamikaze fishing", 149
kayaks, 125, 126, 128, 129, 130
    as camouflage, 126
Key Largo, Florida, 128
Killian, Bill, 127, 143, 147
Knighten, Capt. George, 68, 182
Kreh, Lefty, 124

L

Lafayette, Louisiana, 169
Laguna Madre, 175, 178, 179, 181
Laguna Madre, Upper, 174, 179
Lake Calcasieu, Louisiana, 169, 170
    Commissary Point, 171
    Grand Bayou, 171
    Lambert's Bayou, 171
    Lambert's Bayou Reef, 171
    Turney's Bay, 171
Lake Charles, Louisiana, 141, 170
Lake Guri, Venezuela, 70, 147
largemouth bass, 214
    Florida strain, 209, 212
    lunkers, 211
Line class records, 204
Little Red River, Arkansas, 121, 124
live bait, 73, 103, 132, 148, 160
Louisiana, 112, 134, 140, 141, 144, 153, 158, 170, 185, 187
Louisiana Department of Wildlife and Fisheries, 140, 205
Louisiana Sportsman, 214
Louisiana State University (LSU), 211
Lower Neches Wildlife Management Area, 184
lures, 72, 73, 132
    grubs, 146
    hard plastic, 149
    Jigging spoons, 147
    soft plastic, 65, 132, 146, 163, 165

M

Mahoney, Timothy, 169
Mansfield Mauler, 181
Marine Gene Probe Laboratory, 211
Maryland, 211
Masson, Todd, 214
Matagorda, Texas, 184
Meacom's Pier, 165
Mighty-Mite anchor, 140
MirrOlure, 63, 149
    Top Dog, 136, 182
    Top Dog Jr., 182
Mississippi, 153, 185
Mississippi Department of Wildlife, Fisheries, and Parks, 205
monofilament, 66, 69, 70, 71, 147
Montgomery, Alabama, 205
Moore, Chester Jr., xiii
Moore, Frank, 67
mud minnows, 166, 184
mullet, 112, 182, 211
    finger, 160

N

National Wildlife Refuge, 185
netting, 187
night fishing, 140
Norton Sand Eel, 169, 182

O

Oakes, Capt. Buddy, 170
oil platforms, 143, 147
Orange County Association for Retarded Children, 179
oxygen, 188
Oyster Lake (Palacious Bayou), 185
oyster reefs, 22

P

P-Line flourocarbon-coaded lines, 69

CXX X-TRA Strong, 70, 147
Palacios, Texas, 184
peacock bass, 65, 70, 147
pelagic species, 142
Persohn, Joe, 161
pier fishing, 155, 164, 165
piggy Perch, 135, 148, 183
Pike, Doug, x
plastic worms, 72
pogey, 160
points, 155, 157
pompano, southern, 147
popping corks, 134, 135, 165
Port Aransas, Texas, 131, 211
Port Arthur, Texas, 177
Port Mansfield, Texas, 181
Port O'Connor, 126
Power Pro fishing lines, 66
Pyle, Capt. Daniel, 44, 145, 177, 178

R

rainbow trout, 124
rainforest, 147
Rat-L-Trap, 133
red drum, 126
red snapper, 74, 147, 189
redfish, 74, 126, 142, 158, 163, 167
rip tides, 138
Rising, Kelly, 177
Rodgers, Stan, 128
Rollover Pass, Galveston, 166, 168, 182, 183
Rue, Capt. Erik, 171

S

Sabine jetties, 131, 139, 140, 143, 178
Sabine Lake, 66, 177
    Coffee Ground Cove, 178
    East Pass, 178
Sabine National Wildlife Refuge, 121
Sabine Pass, 70, 141, 145, 148, 153, 154

Index

Sabine Snake, 182
salmonids, 211
Saltwater Assassins, 182
sand eels, 22
sandbars, 155, 157, 158
Sciaenidae, 1
Sea & Sea MX-10 underwater camera, 151
shad, 166, 179
Shakespeare, 132
    Ugly Stik, 132
ShareLunker program, 212
sharks, 74, 142, 145, 148, 158, 163
Shaunessy, Capt. Terry, 69
sheepshead, 142, 147
shoreline, 155, 157, 182, 183
short rigs, 143, 144, 146, 147, 152, 206, 214
shrimp, 165, 191
    dead shrimp, 134, 166
    Galveston Bay, 171
    live shrimp, 134, 147, 166, 171
    Trinity Bay, 171
shrimp tails, 165
Slimy Slugs, 149
Smith's Point, 172
South America, 65
South Florida, 69
South Pass jetties, 131
South Texas, 178
Spanish mackerel, 142, 148
Speck Rigs, 165
Speck-Tacular Trout Adventures, 135
speckled trout. See spotted seatrout
Spell, Charles, 147
Spider Fusion, 66
Spiderwire, 66
Spiller, Kyle, 174, 175
spoons, 64, 72, 161, 187
spotted seatrout, x, 1, 66, 68, 70, 131, 145, 151, 155, 160, 166, 169, 170, 171, 172, 175, 176, 178, 181, 183, 187, 201, 204, 206, 209, 211, 212
    Alabama state record, 206
    Florida state record, 206
    fly-fishing for, 121-130
    Freezing, 189
    genetic altering, 210
    INFORMATION RESOURCES ON THE WEB, 206
    keeping alive, 188
    Louisiana state record, 206
    Mississippi state record, 206
    nutrition, 212
    radio telemetry, 210
    recipes, 191
        Baked trout in Garlic and Olive Oil, 200
        Baked Trout With Seafood, 191
        Barbecued Speckled Trout, 191
        Beer Batter Fish Fry, 199
        Boiled Speckled Trout, 197
        Crabby Stuffed Trout, 196
        Herbed Trout With Sour Cream, 192
        Kennet Fried Trout, 192
        Sesame Fried Trout, 193
        Sourdough Stuffed Trout, 194
        Thyme Trout, 197
        Trout Amandine with Creole Sauce, 198
        Trout and Sour Cream, 194
        Trout Italian, 195
        Trout Spaghetti, 198
        Trout with Bananas, 200
        Trout With Horseradish Sauce, 195
    record books, 201
    Super Trout, 209
    Tagging studies, 210
    Texas state record, 172, 206
    world record, 206
State Highway 35, 185

State Highway 87, 183, 184
State Line Guide Service, 145
Stateline Guide Service, 177
stingrays, 142, 163, 177
Stren, 70
    Sensor monofilament line, 70
Structure, 145, 158, 176
sublimation, 189
Super Spook, 136
surf fishing, 155, 158, 163, 187
    bowls, 157
    guts, 157
    pockets, 157
    rims, of surf bowls, 157
    safety, 163
    teacup formations, 157
    troughs, 157
Surfside jetties, 131

T

Tabasco, 191
Tackle, 61
    Fly-fishing Gear, 123
        Flies, 121
            Bay Anchovy, 124
            Clouser Minnow, 121, 124, 129
            Deceiver Menhaden, 124
            Deer Hair Mullet, 124
            Lefty's Deceiver, 124
            Poppers, 124
        leader, fly, 203
        line, fly, 203
        reels, fly, 203
        rods, fly, 121, 123, 129, 203
    for jetties, 132
    hooks, 72
        4/0, 72
        circle, 74, 148
        J-style, 72, 148
        Japanese, 74

        Kahle-style, 72, 148
        treble, 73
    leaders, steel, 148
    line, 61, 62, 66
    lines, braided, 66, 69, 147
    lines, fluorocarbon, 69
    lines, fusion, 66, 69
    lines, super , 66, 68
    reel spools, 69
    reels, 61, 64, 141, 187
        bait-casting , 62, 132, 137
        spinning , 62, 66, 69, 72
    rods, 61, 65, 137, 141, 187
        choosing, 64
        fiberglass, 65
        graphite, 65
        heavy action, 64
        light action, 64
        popping, 143
        surf, 158, 163
Tallahassee, Florida, 205
Texas City flats, 172
Texas City, Texas, 172
Texas Coastal Bend, 173, 178
Texas Department of Agriculture, 202
Texas Fish & Game magazine, 70
Texas Outdoor Writers Association, ix
Texas Parks & Wildlife Department (TPWD), †4, 73, 173, 174, 201, 202, 203, 204, 205, 206, 211, 212, 214
    Texas Gulf Coast Roundup, 212
thawing frozen seafood, 190
Thibodeaux, Mack, 160, 161
tides, 206
    charts, 166, 206
topwater, 68, 73, 181, 182
topwater plugs, 65, 68, 136
Tough Line fishing line, 66
Tres Palacios Bay, 185
Triple Fish monofilament line, 70
trolling motors, 32, 127, 151

Index

Trout hotspots, 169
tube jigs, 64
Turtle Bayou, 185

U

U.S. Army Corps of Engineers, 163
undertows, 138
University of Texas Marine Science Center, 211
Upper Texas Coast, 144

V

Venezuela, 70, 147

W

wade-fishing, 126, 178, 182
waders, 163
Wallace, Jim, 172, 178, 207
West, Craig, 173
Wester, Jay, 177
white bass, 134
whitetailed deer, 212
wind, 153
Worcestershire sauce, 199